Digital Citizenship for Children and Youths

Seda Gökçe Turan

Digital Citizenship for Children and Youths

**Bibliographic Information published by the
Deutsche Nationalbibliothek**
The Deutsche Nationalbibliothek lists this publication in the Deutsche
Nationalbibliografie; detailed bibliographic data is available online at
http://dnb.d-nb.de.

Library of Congress Cataloging-in-Publication Data
A CIP catalog record for this book has been applied for at the
Library of Congress.

This publication was printed with the support of Bahçeşehir University.

Cover illustration: © Monkey Business Images/shutterstock.com

ISBN 978-3-631-82792-5 (Print)
E-ISBN 978-3-631-84352-9 (E-PDF)
E-ISBN 978-3-631-84353-6 (EPUB)
E-ISBN 978-3-631-84354-3 (MOBI)
DOI 10.3726/b17915

© Peter Lang GmbH
Internationaler Verlag der Wissenschaften
Berlin 2021
All rights reserved.

Peter Lang – Berlin · Bern · Bruxelles · New York · Oxford · Warszawa · Wien

All parts of this publication are protected by copyright. Any
utilisation outside the strict limits of the copyright law, without
the permission of the publisher, is forbidden and liable to
prosecution. This applies in particular to reproductions,
translations, microfilming, and storage and processing in
electronic retrieval systems.

This publication has been peer reviewed.

www.peterlang.com

Preface

It is so obvious that all parents and teachers have great concern about technology usage, harms and risks of technology and digital environments. When they focus on risks and harms, sometimes they can miss the actual point that technology and Internet usage is not a choice or option. In the 21st century, every citizen should have competences about digital worlds. Of course, there are risks in the digital world, but we have to teach to ourselves and children how to manage and handle those risks. Digital citizenship seems like a solution.

I hope this book will help teachers, parents and youths to survive in the digital world and benefit from it.

Seda Gökçe Turan
İstanbul, 2020

Content

Introduction 9

1. Children and Youths in Digital Environments 13
1.1. Children and Youths' Digital Environment Usage Habits and Online Behaviors 16

2. Risks and Benefits of Digital Environments 21
2.1. Benefits of Digital Environments 21
2.1.1. Educational Technology 22
2.1.2. Digital Identity Development of Children and Youths 24
2.2. Risks of Digital Environment 26
2.2.1. Media Manipulation 27
2.2.2. Cyber-Bullying 31
2.2.2.1. Effects of Cyber-Bullying 35
2.2.2.2. Preventing Cyber-Bullying 37
2.2.3. Technoference 39

3. Digital Citizenship 41
3.1. Respect Yourself/Respect Others 43
3.1.1. Digital Access 43
3.1.2. Digital Etiquette 47
3.1.3. Digital Law 48
3.2. Educate Yourself/Connect with Others 49
3.2.1. Digital Literacy 49
3.2.1.1. Media Literacy 50
3.2.1.2 Digital Media Literacy 61
3.2.2. Digital Communication 68
3.2.3. Digital Commerce 70

3.3. Protect Yourself/Protect Others 71
　　3.3.1. Digital Rights and Responsibilities 71
　　3.3.2. Digital Security (Self-Protection) 73
　　3.3.3. Digital Health and Wellness 73

Conclusion 75

References 77

Introduction

Although the 21st century is known by many different names (Digital Age, Age of Technology, Age of Artificial Intelligence, etc.), it has diverse characteristics and easy access to "information" (Koltay, 2011). The impact of information on individuals and societies could be very diverse due to the structure of information in the 21st century. With different information and communication devices and digital environments, information could be both beneficial and dangerous. For example, information can be replaced with artificial intelligence applications such as Deep Fake, and it is so difficult for children and youths to differentiate Deep Fake from real ones. Moreover, parents and teachers are supposed to direct and guide children and youths for safe and conscious Internet use. But unfortunately, most of the time they are not aware of the harms and dangers on the Internet. That's why we need to teach not only to children and youths but also to parents and teachers the digital citizenship skills so that children and youths can adapt to social life, living in a safe society, to make them conscious citizens, and to teach our children and youths some skills in schools to make them aware of the risks of the cyber world, while making them benefit from cyber world. In order to do this, parents and teachers, first focus equally on the risks and benefits of the cyber world, become conscious digital citizens, thus being models for children and youths. When we focus only on the risks (cyber-bullying, Internet addiction, hate speech, technoference, etc.) in the cyber world, we deprive not only children and youths but also adults from this world, which facilitate our daily lives, can benefit for our intellectual development, offer opportunities to have fun, easily communicate with people in different countries and follow and learn what is going on in the world. Not only for children, youths or adults but also for elders, there are ambivalent discussions. According to the findings, although they are exposed to fraud in cyber space and can believe very easily in fake news, social media is also presented as a factor that reduces anxiety for elders and increases their quality of life satisfaction and happiness (Chen & Schultz, 2016; Abad, 2014). Similarly, social media defined as "second life place" is not only for children and youths but also for elder people and adults, and it is kind of a routine part of daily life (Hallam & Zanella, 2017). Especially at social network sites, users and individuals are defined as a population, and they play a crucial role due to their effect on establishing and reinforcing social norms (Hallam & Zanella, 2017). When looking at news spreading on social media, stories of victims of cyber-bullying or websites that tell them about the impact of fake news on children and youths, parents' concerns seem normal. But the point is we should not forget that just as we are likely to be snatched by thieves in daily life, but of course we do not stop going outside and taking our children outside, we should not stop joining cyber world as well.

In terms of harms and risks of digital environments, researchers (Jones & Mitchell, 2016) argued that instead of directly informing children and youths of dark sides of the Internet like cyber-bullying, sexting, online harassment, Internet addiction, etc., we should gain them digital citizenship skills and competence, so they would have chance to practice about showing respectful behaviors during online disagreement, taking others' perspectives, and standing by people who were abused online as a result of those behaviors and practices; and there would be a possibility to reduce cyber harassment.

Before examining the digital citizenship in depth, there are some core questions that should be answered such as the meaning of living in a media culture and digital society, the expectations and perception of individuals toward digitalized and mediated society, the meaning of media and digital world for schools and institutions and parents and teachers perception about digital education as well. For this reason, approaches toward digital citizenship could not be considered without sociological, psychological and cultural aspects, dimensions and dynamics.

The definition of "digital citizenship" is also another important point. At formal education schools, teachers and practitioners give importance to educate pupils for national norms and enable them to become conscious citizens, who are aware of their responsibilities and rights; actively participate in society and obey the rules and obligations. So, there are some questions that we should answer in order to make clear definition of digital citizenship, such as do traditional or offline citizenship remain the same at the digitalized society? Are there differences between online and offline citizenship? Is this clue for catching antisocial and psychopaths to break the laws in digital environments? Are trolls a danger for offline society? (Choi et al., 2018).

To sum up, researchers strongly advise to improve individual's digital citizenship competencies (Xu et al., 2019; Jones & Mitchell, 2016). Technical skill s such as accessing Internet and using technological devices are necessary but not enough for safe engagement in the digital world (Choi et al., 2018). Children and youths should have competences to search and obtain information and gain awareness not only on local but also global levels. Furthermore, children and youths should have the chance to get actively involved in digital environments, such as communicating, cooperating and collaborating with others. As educators, parents and researchers, we should understand children and youths' education and competence of social media and other digital media environments.

In this book, I tried to figure out features and characteristics of cyber world in terms of children and youths' engagement in digital environments. Only talking about harms, risks and dangers of digital environment is useless for the digital age. We should encourage children and youths for active participation while teaching how to protect themselves from dark sides of digital environment.

1. Children and Youths in Digital Environments

As underlined in most of the studies (Hallam & Zanella, 2017; Subrahmanyam & Greenfiled, 2008), digital environments are not only places that children and youths only spend time. Indeed, they are "living" in digital environments; they learn, share and teach something and present their lives to others. Moreover, even children and youths interact with their social and political environment by digital tools and platforms. Politics are not too far away issues for children and youths as a result of engagement in digital environments. Unfortunately, they can encounter political information which is mostly not appropriate with their age, cognition level or background information. Those encounters can be evaluated as dark side on Internet and social media.

It is a fact that social media network sites have great impact on both online and offline lives of individuals and are changing social dynamics as well. Especially by facing and interacting with unfamiliar people, perceptions, thoughts or beliefs on social media network sites, youths and young adults have a chance to practice and build their identity (Hallam & Zanella, 2017).

According to the findings of EU Kids Online, which is systematic research on media use habits of children and adolescence since 2010 among European Countries (Rasi et al., 2019), there are some vital conclusions about relationship between children and adolescents and digital environments. Firstly, there is a positive correlation between children and youths' Internet usage and improvement of their digital skills. This means that in order to improve children and youths' digital skills, we should offer them opportunity for Internet access. But, according to the findings of EU Kids Online, not all Internet engagements are beneficial for children and youths. However, not all risks of Internet are related with harm or abuse. In order to provide Internet safety and conscious Internet usage, parents, teachers and education commission members are so important for constructing not only an education system but also educational policies (Livingstone, 2019).

In order to deeply analyze children and youths' digital environment enrollment, developmental characteristics of children and youths should be evaluated. As known, most of the behaviors of children and youths could be defined and explained by some key words characterized by their developmental stages. Those concepts are like identity, autonomy, privacy and sexuality. On the other hand, developmental changes that depend on the adolescence period or cognitive development, gender or social-economic status also affect children and youths' behaviors. For the 21st century, it could be said that digital environment engagement also effects the development of children and youths. At the digital world, virtual world and real world are linked together and this link effect individuals' identity, sexuality and politic perception and development in real world (Valenzuela et al., 2012; Ahn, 2011). There are variety of studies about children's and youths' digital involvement. While some studies focus on online and offline communication and their characteristics, the others focus on the effect of online engagement on children and youths' identity development (James & Cotnam-Kappel, 2020; Sugihartati, 2019). Despite all the discussions, there is a consensus that digital environments present another and symbolic world to children and youths. So, how do children and youths spend time in this symbolic world? Moreover, is this a "symbolic" world or real world for children and youths?

Digital environments are areas that present attractive subjects, forums and fun-entertainments. At digital platforms, users especially prefer social media network sites such as Twitter, Instagram, YouTube or Facebook. Besides those social network sites, blogs and vlogs are so popular among youths and teenagers (DePaula et al., 2018; Valkenburg & Peter, 2007).

At digital platforms, teenagers and youths could participate in discussions about health and hot topics related to current issues or general disclosures (Saud et al., 2020). Another advantage of digital platforms is it offers youths with HIV, eating disorders or low self-esteem a chance to talk their issues freely. Some youths with cancer create blog or vlog and talk about their diseases and they report that it makes them better emotionally (McGillivray et al., 2016; Subrahmanyam & Greenfield, 2008).

Apart from getting information about health issues, youths and adolescents have questions about sexuality, and they feel free when they ask them on digital environments anonymously (Yeo & Chu, 2017). According to findings (Yeo & Chu, 2017) that examined a popular health webpage, there are very surprising results. Researchers noted that teenagers feel free at discussions about adolescent health and sexual health. Moreover, teenagers reported that they get emotional support by other users. For developing countries, due to lack of health services, those type of web pages would be more beneficial (Subrahmanyam & Greenfield, 2008). Researchers (Mitchell et al., 2007) noted that with better education and law rules on Internet, it could be possible to reduce unwanted sexual talking in digital environments, which was proved by teenagers and adolescence who are digitally literate and aware of their rights, and they reported that they are less subject to dirty talking or sexting on digital environments.

For dirty talking or abusive disclosures, youths mostly reported rude interpretations, make shame users about their sharing and talking about sex with strangers. Youths who experienced online verbal abuse reported that they experienced emotional stress and depressive symptoms and were subject to offline verbal abuse (Ashiekpe & Ugande, 2017).

It is obvious that digital environments have both positive and negative impact on children and youths' psychology, mental health and mood. Especially feedbacks from other users could have an impact on self-confidence of youths and adolescence (McLean et al., 2019).

While analyzing social media effect on children and youths, there is a vital point that is not to be forgotten: Developmental characteristics. Especially in teenage period, those characters become more visible. One of the most apparent characteristics of teenage period is romantic relationships. Teenagers mostly give importance to their physical appearance, being attractive to the opposite sex. Findings showed that teenagers use social media and other digital environments in order to strengthen their romantic relationships. According to findings, teenagers and youths could pursue their online relationships, which started in social dating sites and social media as face-to-face relationships (Abbasi, 2019; Seidman et al., 2019). Those findings are so important because they also clarify the motivation of youths to use social media. Youths are also at-risk groups for cyberstalking, dating abuse and cyber-fraud because they have not enough experience and not cognitively mature; these characteristics lead to risky situations. Implication of cyber flirting and romantic relationships is sometimes unfortunately "cyberstalking," which is defined as all forms of stalking by using information and communication technologies that include any actions to thread that aim to victim distress (Bocij, 2004). Cyberstalking also includes behaviors tracing both online and offline environments, getting information about victims' personal and private lives. According to findings (DreBing et al, 2014; Reed et al., 2016), cyberstalking is so common among university students. In addition to cyberstalking, digital dating abuse, which is defined as abusive behaviors by existing or former partners or flirts such as controlling, repression or thread through technological devices, is also common among youths and teenagers. That digital dating abuse is one of the most negative consequences of talking and meeting strangers at online platforms.

Now, children's and youths' online behaviors and their effect on their whole development will be discussed.

1.1. Children's and Youths' Digital Environment Usage Habits and Online Behaviors

New technologies especially social network sites submit a variety of opportunities for users to express themselves, share personal information and encounter different thoughts, ideas and beliefs (Hallam & Zanella, 2017). Generally, as researchers, educators and policy makers we should aim to teach children and youths to behave in a safe and responsible way on digital environments. Respectful behaviors seem as a first step for contribution to well-being of society or community and ability to tolerance for different perspectives and thoughts that children and youths encounter in digital environments frequently (Jones & Mitchell, 2016).

Both traditional media and digital environments shape behaviors of users. There are some dimensions for this shaping effects.

Social relationship seems like an important value for social network sites by users. With the social reward or built connection with friends, family or friends of friends, acquaintances, users feel they get in touch with other people and they get motivated for being socially active online (Dannels & Vanwynberghe, 2017; Hallam & Zanella, 2017).

Researchers (Hintz et al., 2017; Lyon, 2017) also discussed about digital culture and society as an increased "surveillance" culture. In this surveillance world, one of the basic characteristics is users actively participate in order to regulate their own surveillance and surveillance of others (Lyon, 2017). Moreover, in this culture the concepts of ethics, rights, political participation and citizenship must be defined again. Because those concepts affects users' thoughts and behaviors not only in digital environments but also in daily lives.

The concerns of parents, educators and researchers generally focus on social media usage habits and behaviors in digital environments of children and youths rather than the usage of the digital tools. The most frequently used digital environment is social media network sites. Of course, social media network sites have different features, but generally, they are similar. Social media network sites are characterized mainly by three domains: (1) Communication through social media does not depend on any institution because it offers opportunity to users to choose their own communication channels; (2) Social media is composed of users-generated content, so message receivers also become message senders; (3) Communication via social media is interactive and could pursue by other networks. Those characteristics of social media are centered mainly on the structure of social media and communication (Zolkepli & Kamarulzaman, 2015; Chan-Olmsted et al., 2013). So, among many other characteristics, social media could have a great impact on children's and youth's communication skills. Moreover, online communication is very beneficial for youths who have difficulty with offline communication. By the way, sometimes, as a developmental stage characteristic, some youths' difficulty with offline communication is so normal. For this difficulty, online communication would make easier those communications and encourage youths' self-esteem (Valkenburg & Peter, 2011).

Digital environments' integrated and penetrated structure creates digital footprints by users when they explore the digital world. Also, those digital footprints give opportunities to users to influence and effect social and political norms with constructing and sharing information (Alvermann & Sanders, 2019). Those digital interactions are not only depending on the digital activities of users but also their knowledge and behavior (Atif & Chou, 2018). In other words, digital footprints and individuals' impact on political and social norms could not be think without their knowledge and both online and offline behaviors.

Furthermore, with improved digital citizenship skills, children and youths have chance to practice in responsible ways toward both themselves and others (Choi et al., 2018).

As seen, in a complex digital world, in order to survive, children and youths should learn digital literacy and have chance to practice to their digital abilities (McGillivray et al., 2019). Because, at digital age, boundaries between offline and online world become more transparent; in terms of children's and youths' online engagement they change and alter their behaviors, face with others from different cultures and society and integrate their online and offline social world (Choi, 2016; Boyd, 2014).

While some researchers claim (Zolkepli & Kamarulzaman, 2015) that the characters presented in media are seen as a role model for children and youths and it effects their learning process, the others (Hogue & Mills, 2019; Huesmann, 2007) even positive or negative, those characters have impact on attitudes, values and behaviors of children and youth. Technology penetrates individuals' lives and becomes essential, for years after 2010s individuals turn to technophile (Benedikter & Fitz, 2011). Technophilia is defined as too much admiration for technology and its benefits (Barrientos- Gutierrez, Lozano, Arillo-Santillan, Morello, Mejia and Thrasher, 2019). Of course, technology is beneficial for both society and individuals, but technophile could be a risk for missing the harms of technology. Different from this argument, Steinerman et al. (2013) stated that when technophile comes together with social heredity, individuals tend to be participants in scientific research or experiments about technological invention. So, individuals, especially children and youths, could give more importance to technology and social media than it deserves. It leads to media and technology manipulation and indirectly effect users' thoughts, believes and behaviors.

As noted, media and technology have great impact on social relationships on individuals' both offline and online behaviors. Furthermore, media has impact on how individuals learn the world and how to interact with each other. This means that mass media is strongly related with individuals' social relationships (Peng et al., 2017).

Today, the 21st century is defined as "Information Society" also. Within this information society, to construct, develop and reinforce attitudes mass media is a priority. But, although it has positive impact on attitudes of individuals, for some people television seems as a "bad guy" for individuals.

Moreover, there are some pathological situations not only for traditional mass media but also for social media usage. For example, it's just a pathological state of fascination unlike admiring a series or a famous artist. Pathological admiration is defined in two ways: obsessively tracking and bothered on social media. Similarly, pathological admiration could be seemed in groups and those people can play role to spread violence, alienation and cult behaviors on media. In the 1990s, the pathological admiration is discussed through television programs, and artists continue to increase with the influence of the Internet and social media. Gans (2014) have a different argument about media and pathology. Gans (2014) claimed that it is not possible to attribute a long-term lasting effect to any content that is offered by media tools. But, unfortunately, media-addicted individuals' minds, cognition and emotions are shaped and influenced by media, and it leads to negative effects on individuals' behaviors, attitudes, beliefs and values. Not only for media-addicted people but also for non-addicted people, media has great impact in terms of their behaviors and attitudes (Gans, 2014).

Moreover, not only actively effects of media but also the "presentation" of children and youths' are the main problem for the harmful effects of media (Ciboci, 2019). Especially for discussions about children, violence and media, the presentation of children on media is a serious problem because they present mostly with victims of war, poverty, abuse and TV shows that include competition, emotional exploitation and circulation or rating anxiety. In order to clarify the effects of media on children and youths, firstly we should accept that media is not purely good or bad. But the individual's usage aims could be classified as good or bad. Some researchers argue that media cultivate ideological ideas, empty satisfactions and narcissistic feelings instead of providing information and enlightenment of individuals (Seidman et al., 2019). We will discuss this topic in depth under the subtitle of "media manipulation."

Valkenburg and Peter (2011) noted that individuals who oppose the authority or have difficulty with authority experience a sense of satisfaction when they see the humiliation of authoritarian figures through media. Moreover, those people have empathy over the figures or characters presented in the media, and they have chance to see the mistakes of others and also have opportunity to see role models in order to imitate. Not only by offering figures and characteristics that individuals imitate, through news and show programs media could affect and direct individuals' mind, perception and social perception as well (Güven, 2015).

Media has five types of effects on individuals: (1) *Behavioral impact*, if individuals perform some behaviors offered by media messages; (2) *Attitudinal impact*, if messages shape individuals' beliefs and values; (3) *Cognitive impact*, if messages shape individuals' thought; (4) *Emotional impact*, if messages effect individuals' anxiety, enthusiasm, joy, and sadness; (5) *Physical impact*, if changes occur in the arousal and other physical reactions of individuals through media messages (Ulaş et al., 2012).

Besides negative effects of media on society and individuals, it is seen that violence in society is increasingly reflected in the media, when think that the media is the mirror of society. As seen from newspapers, there was a significant increase in news related to violence at schools between the 1990s and 2000s (Teyfur, 2014). Not only news but also cartoons are seemed as a negative and inappropriate role model for children. Although some researchers advise video games and cartoons that they believe violence is part of real life, children and youths should be familiar with it, and most of the researchers believe it could lead to desensitization toward violence (Temizyürek & Acar, 2014). According to studies about most popular cartoons Teletubbies and Smurfs as examined via semiology, those cartoons have subliminal messages about sex, death and violence (Temizyürek & Acar, 2014). In my opinion, sometimes both researchers and parents could exaggerate "subliminal" messages of cartoons and behave too sensitive about this. Not all cartoons or films have dangers, violence or death concepts for kids. Moreover, kids are not so sensitive about those concepts most of the times. Sometimes they are unconscious about those concepts and only enjoy the cartoons.

While research into the effects of traditional media on individuals continues, with the creation and spread of Facebook in 2004, studies have started to be conducted on the individual effects of social media. Studies about social media generally focus on the question "Is social media a tool, a venue, a content or a type of communication?" But, unfortunately rapid changes on digitalization negatively affect studies about social media. So, clear and subtle results and decisions about effects of social media on individuals especially children and youth are not trustable (Komaya, 2012).

Medina and her team's (2014) project study titled "Social Reality Configurations of University Students in Honduras on Facebook" is one of the comprehensive studies on this topic. This study was carried out between 2011 and 2012 with the participation of 250 university students between the ages of 18 and 24. The purpose of the research is to discuss privacy policies in the use of Facebook, what impacts or ness of these policies are in users' publishing, how they shape users' virtual identities and whether Facebook is the ideal environment for communication. In this context, participants' Facebook usage habits and profiles were examined in terms of different variables. As a result of the research, participants spent more than an hour a day on Facebook. In this process, it was determined that they communicate mainly (70%), communicate with friends, share photos and videos, and communicate with family. 80.1% of respondents said they used their real names on Facebook. However, when people tried to access their Facebook account, it was found that they either used only one name or used their first and second names, so it was difficult for participants to identify on Facebook. 75.3% of respondents said they did not share their private information on Facebook. However, when their profile pages were examined, it was seen that their date of birth, place of residence, telephone numbers, e-mail addresses and other information that could be considered personal information were published. The concept of "friendship" was not clear in terms of participants in the context of social media. 81.7% of respondents said they set the privacy settings on their Facebook profiles to "Only my friends can see it." However, 89.2% of respondents said they met face-to-face with their "friends" on Facebook at least once, while 54.3% said there were people on Facebook who could not identify as "friends" in everyday life, while 55% said the number of friends on Facebook was greater than the number of friends in daily life. Sixty-two percent of respondents said they thought their Facebook profile was the appropriate means to tell others who they really were. Those results are very important to evaluate media and social media effects on children's and youths' behaviors.

To conclude, it is obvious that traditional and digital media have great impact on children's and youths' minds, thoughts, attitudes and behaviors. Now, we should discuss about risks and benefits of digital environments, which are direct issues about digital citizenship.

2. Risks and Benefits of Digital Environments

2.1. Benefits of Digital Environments

Although most researchers, educators, policymakers discuss and warn about harms, risks and deleterious effects of digital environments, I should note that digital environments are one of the best tools to shape individuals lives and perception toward other people and to expand their circle of friends and acquaintances, developing healthy identity, etc. Mainly social network sites encourage three basic individual needs: (1) diversion and entertainment, (2) development of identity and support personal growth and autonomy and (3) build and maintain social relationships (Hallam & Zanella, 2017).

Although children and youths could face with different political disclosures on social media, researchers noted that (Atif & Chou, 2018) social media could reinforce their genuine learning experiences through reflective and critical discussions on social media.

Moreover, active engagement of digital world and improved digital competences are considered as key qualifications for lifelong learning (Rasi et al., 2019). For this reason, researchers strongly advise active engagement of children and youths in the digital world. This active engagement could offer opportunities such as be informed, present and express themselves and encourage the feeling of safety. Furthermore, the most important benefit of actively using digital tools is to support and improve individuals' problem-solving capabilities.

Generally, parents and sometimes teachers are worried about children and youths to consume their time playing digital games on the Internet. They mostly think playing digital games could lead to game addiction, academic unsuccess or poor social relationships. There are also studies about relationship between digital game addiction and cyber-bullying. For example, Chang et al. (2015) noted that playing digital game, exposed to media violence, risky Internet usage and engagement with cyber-bullying both as a victim or perpetrator, is related with being cyber-bullying and cyber-victimization. But, indeed researchers (Dezuanni, 2018; Dezuanni et al., 2015; Pellicone & Ahn, 2015) claim just the opposite. Digital games or online games have positive impacts and provide potential for education of children. Of course, pathological playing, isolation or showing psychological symptoms while playing online games are indicators of problems and should be handled by professionals. This is another subject and not so common. But, using digital games as a reward or part of education could provide an opportunity to support children's and youth's development and academic success. Moreover, digital games like Minecraft, which enable users to interact with each other simultaneously or through YouTube channels about the games, offer chance to them to support their social participation and social relationships. Those results might reduce parents concerns about their childrens social relationships. Again, it should be underlined that both children and youths should support digital games, social media usage and face-to-face communication.

There are benefits of digital environment in this book, those benefits will be discussed under two sections in this chapter: Education Technology and Digital Identity. The other benefits like strengthening social and romantic relationships, accessing easily information and encountering different perspectives and ideas were discussed under different topics in this book.

2.1.1. Educational Technology

Like all other part of life and society, education is affected by digital technology and its impact. It is so cliché, but students K-12 can access networks, technological devices and Internet in their homes, bedrooms and across the world. They have access to the Internet free from time and space. So, it is obvious that for digital age, integrating technology to all steps and classes of education is not only a choice but also mandatory.

Besides using technological devices in educational context, educators tend to use social media and other digital environments like digital games in order to support pupils' learning not only in schools but beyond the schoolyards. Moreover, technological devices and platforms are also used for sharing and presenting pupils' term papers or homework, which increase participations and social relationships of pupils (McGillivray et al., 2016; Boyd, 2014).

Digital education is mostly referred to as the process of teaching and learning about digital technology and the use of digital technology in educational spaces (Emejulu & McGregor, 2019). To develop digital citizenship competencies of kids and pupils, the role of distance education and pedagogical methods and practices, which also encourage digital media literacy skills of students, should not be ignored. Moreover, distance education is also an opportunity to reduce the gap between students who have chance to access computers and do not have any chances. But unfortunately, it is only valid for social governments who have role to offer computers to their students. For capitalist societies, distance education is very difficult for students who do not have chance to access either computer or Internet. Additionally, for those pupils, distance education is not beneficial because they are not benefitting from face-to-face education effectively. Basically, they cannot do their homework that are on digital environments.

For school-aged children, transform digital practices into educational curriculum evaluated as an opportunity for pupils in order to harness the benefits and opportunities of digital environments and gain students' awareness about harms and risks of virtual spaces. According to the findings, technological accessibility of students is important to improve their digital citizenship competence, and educators should be aware of their transformational roles (Atif & Chou, 2018).

Mostly, because of lack of information about the digital world, parents and educators focus on risks and harms of it. But distance education offers online learning opportunities not only for children and youths but also for parents and educators (Rasi et al., 2019). As noted by different researchers (Choi et al., 2018) in order to improve digital citizenship competences and skills of children and youths, parents and educators should have improved digital citizenship competences. So, in order to improve digital citizenship skills distance education would be a great opportunity.

It is obvious that education is digitalized. In the 21st century, especially university students mostly choose to take note digitally. They did not use traditional methods like pencil and paper. It is believed that for the further years for primary schools or high schools, pupils prefer taking notes digitally and use laptops or tablets. Especially university students reported that they found taking digital notes and using technological devices better for reading handwriting and reducing spelling error. But there are also disadvantages like distractibility and plagiarism (Tüzel & Tok, 2013). Moreover, university students in the field of computer teaching defined digital media literacy skills better then media literacy skills. But unfortunately, they could not have skills related to searching and syntheses different data sources (Coşkun et al., 2013).

Researchers suggest that social media and higher education are coactive strength that influences human behavior and development. For this reason, there is a strong relationship between peoples' competence of using social media and social, political and pedagogical parts of technology usage. Also, the individuals' level of digital citizenship effects all aspects of participation in the digital world through influencing other users' learning, work performance, personal safety and information security (Jones & Mitchell, 2016).

According to education researchers and politicians, the key factor about improving digital competence is involving in social media. At digital age, children and youths not only spare their time in social media but also create their own blogs, animation games and videos (Kafai & Peppler, 2011). For this reason, some researchers argued that (Baytun & Özerdem, 2012) technology is the vital point in order to meet the necessities of the age and individual's needs, whereas the others claimed that (Wariya, 2016) online puns or word games pedagogically support students' vocab language and grammar skills, so teachers should encourage students to do so.

Society and individuals are subjected to deep and long-term media transformation during the media industry reproduced traditional media products by users (Jenkins & Deuze, 2008). With the pervasive usage of Internet and communication devices, individuals begin to compare digital media products and printed media products. There are similarities and differences between printed and digital media contents. The most obvious difference is digital media contents are composed of codes and those codes offer a dynamic structure for digital contents. In other words, users could interfere and change the products. Moreover, when searching digitally, users can reach the text directly with different words or hints that draw attention, not with a certain word. This reveals the concept of "hypertextuality." The feature of hypertextuality allows users to manipulate not only language-related data but also images, sounds, videos and animations. Amedieu et al. (2015) discussed hypertextuality and its effects on learning performance of students. According to results, there is strong relationship with hypertextual contents and effective, persistent learning of pupils. The effectiveness and persistence of learning depend on other factors such as guidance of teachers and cognitive competence. When students are overloaded and exposed to text "bombs" they had not enough performance. Also, the design of the material is so important for effectiveness of learning and motivation and memory of students.

2.1.2. Digital Identity Development of Children and Youths

It is an undeniable fact that digital environments especially social media network sites have a great impact on children's and youths' lives. With the new tools on social media network sites, users have a chance to construct and maintain relationships, and those relationships are vital for psychosocial development of them (Hallam & Zanella, 2017). Social media, as researchers stressed, offers more opportunity than the offline world for freedom, identity development and maintain social relationships (Daneels & Vanwynberghe, 2017). Especially, for understanding the effects of technological devices and digital environments on children's and youths' online behaviors and communication, we should analyze how technological devices and digital environment influence interpersonal communication and construction of identity.

According to findings (Subrahmanyam & Greenfield, 2008), engagement in the digital environment encourages youths to connect others freely and develop a sense of belonging.

Most of the research foci underline digital citizenship and online civic engagement depending on individual background, psychological characteristics and engagement in digital environments that could vary. Moreover, individual backgrounds such as age, gender and socio-economic status are strongly related with users' technical competences, digital literacy and online political engagement (Choi et al., 2018). Because digital identity could not be evaluated without real-life identity, we must define children's and youths' digital identities.

In order to understand children's and youths' digital identity the role of social media and "presenting" concept should be investigated. It is known that online sharing activities are increased, and they have strong effect on children's and youths' identity development (Hogan, 2010). As a developmental characteristic of teenage period, youths mostly like to share and present their lives to others. On social media profiles, youths mostly present themselves and their lives to their friends from offline world, and other users who they only know from online world. Moreover, social media offers youths to share their status, emotional moods and daily experiences with others. For their platonic love affairs or dating, those sharing romantic relationships provide chance to express themselves. Some youths have difficulty to express themselves as a characteristic of adolescence period. Especially while talking with their partner or dating, they have difficulty more than normal or a bit shy (Middaugh, 2019). But at digital platforms (social media, online games, etc.), youths could pretend like an idealized person, which is a role model for themselves. They behave as if they were at a comfort zone. In addition to this, since for some youth's face-to-face communication especially for romantic relationships it could be very difficult, and some youths feel more comfortable with digital communication. But the key point is how digital environments affect youths' digital identities. Because if the youths get used to digital communication and pretend as if only their digital identity, daily life communication and real relationships would be more difficult for them.

In terms of digital literacy skills, Boyd (2014) noted that there are strong relationship between digital identity development of youths and their digital literacy competences. Because social media are generally characterized with self-shaped environments and users have chance to alter or organize their social media network sites, there is positive correlation between their digital competence and digital identity construction.

In the technology age, it is impossible to think as if our real identity could not affect digital environments. If children and youths can have chance to meet and confront with "healthy" role models for themselves both in offline and online world, undoubtedly, they would have healthy identity development chance. They would not only know "idealized" people but also normal, healthy people who have emotions, angers, sometimes defects, etc. For healthy identity development, children and youths would have chance to learn or know that there are some people in the world who think different from you and it is not to make them "bad" people. Digital environments are best places for youths to experience this idea.

But of course, especially for children and younger teenagers, digital environments are not so "good." There are risks and harms as well. Now, we will turn those matters.

2.2. Risks of Digital Environment

Even digital environments have negative consequences; we live in a digitalized society and unfortunately, some researchers have really great concerns about extremely negative consequences of Internet and digital environments (Choi, 2016). Because mostly stressed the risks and harms in other words the dark side of Internet by researchers, parents have unrealistic and awful scenarios about their children's Internet usage. As a result of those fears, parents try to control, monitor or instruct their children's social media usage and mediate their social media behaviors. Those actions restrict children and youths to involve the digital environment. This restriction also means a lack of benefit from opportunities of the Internet and digital environments (Daneels & Vanwynsberghe, 2017). But, for effective mediation, parents and educators should have digital citizenship competence. Without digital citizenship competence and lack of social media usage, parents and educators would affect speculations rather than scientific proofs about benefits of digital environments. Researchers mostly suggest to parents to improve their media literacy skills and to become able to talk and discuss with their children about their online experiences or anything they watch on television. Those sharing that are available with improved digital citizenship of parents would also improve communication and interaction between parents and children in offline world (Rasi et al., 2019).

Researchers argue that Internet and digital environments are seemed attractive and source for online harassment by perpetrators (Valkenburg & Peter, 2011). First, digital environments are source for perpetrators in order to collect data and harass the victims very easily. The use of all information on users' profiles especially on dating or sexual friend sites makes it easier for abusers to get information about their victims. According to findings, digital environments make it easier to gather information about victims, track and communicate with victims, develop fantasies, overcome suppression, reduce anxiety and communicate with other perpetrators (Ybarra et al., 2007; McGrath & Casey, 2002). Although those sites are considered legal, there was a significant relationship between the use of such sites in Japan in 2002 and the increase in homicides and rapes. Perpetrators also use such sites to valid their own thoughts by meeting people who agree with them, to reach out more victims, and for child pornography. Researchers take into consideration the benefit of information technology devices and are studying harmful consequences for adolescents. Findings showed that elementary and high school pupils are harassed more easily by information technology devices than ever before (Moshfegh & Ebrahimi, 2018).

Now we will deeply analyze risks and harms of digital environments.

2.2.1. Media Manipulation

There are some obvious facts about media and violence or digital harassment. When children and youths watch horror movies or so much blood on TV, directly exposed to hate speech or racism in digital environments, their emotional moods, behaviors or psychologies are directly affected from this violence. But, manipulation of individuals' mind through media or digital environments is much more danger issue. The traces of horror movie or blood or murder at TV can be fixed easier than traces of manipulations. Researchers also stated that innovations and transformation in new media can manipulate "crisis communication" in societies. Especially, twitter, blogs and other social media tools have very important roles in times of crisis (Schultz et al., 2011). But, at the same time those crisis time trolls, media manipulations and fake news also spread very rapidly.

With media manipulations, individuals' perception about their and others' lives would be impressed. Especially for perception delusions about safety concepts such as terror attacks, earthquake, kidnapping, etc., children and youths are more impressed about media contents because they do not have enough "safety" perception (Comer et al., 2008). Because, those manipulations are directly related to individuals' fear of future also.

There is also strong relationship between media and agenda setting, which is also defined with media manipulation. According to findings (Gencer, 2012) individuals' agenda is so similar with the mass media agenda which they are exposed to. Researchers argue that individuals' agenda is not composed without impact of mass media. Not only for adults or university students but also for teenagers and high school students the results about mass media showed that mass media effect their perception toward history or current issues (Şeker & Şimşek, 2012). Moreover, taken into consideration studies about family and mass media, they have similar effects. Individuals thought that TV movies have negative effects on children's psychologies, marriage programs damage the morality of society, TV shows and programs have negative impacts on domestic communication and mass media sets the agenda of individuals and society. In contrast, the others argue that mass media raises awareness in society (Kara, 2011). Some research about mass media does not give hopes with the results that TV reduces pupils' reading habits but increases violence, inappropriate habits and reinforces engagement in crimes or harassment. Not only for TV shows or programs but also for video games there are so many discussions. For example, Cranwell et al. (2016) noted that adolescents exposed to tobacco and alcohol consumption in popular video games are more prone to tobacco and alcohol use. For secondary abuse effect of mass media, there are different studies (Cheng et al., 2016). In the studies after Tsunami in Japan, researchers noted that individuals who were not directly exposed to tsunami and learned from TV were more affected by tsunami. But social media had more effect on individuals who directly exposed to tsunami (Cheng et al., 2016). Establishing a positive connection between families and the community and the media, it has been found to be very effective in terms of accelerating civil communication, taking more altruistic actions and taking measures for potential disasters in the future.

There is a significant difference between TV environment and real world. Moreover, individuals also think real-world experiences and TV programs are so different (Narmanlıoğlu, 2016). In order to understand differences between symbolic and real world, Gerbners' Cultivation Theory should be analyzed in depth.

Gerbner (1970: 69) argued that the media creates a new symbolic environment, which aims to create three basic formations, drawing attention to the quality of life of individuals, people's predispositions to shaping and policies for society: Institutions, messages and society. In this context, Gerbner and his team (1969) have started their long-term and broad-based projects, which describe the "Cultural Indicators." Within the scope of the project, first, corporate processes analyses were conducted, and messages of mass media were evaluated in terms of corporate structures, power balances and decision-making processes of individuals. Secondly, message system analyses were conducted, and it was revealed how to cluster patterns with the comprehensive structure in the messages. In the third part of the study, corporate process, message systems and perception of society were examined within the interactions of cultivations effects (Morgan ve Shanahan, 2010). Gerbner (1970) stated that his discussion about "cultivation" is not directly related with knowledge, education, convincing or effects of direct communication, but directly related with how individuals and society interpret and react. Gerbner (1970) thinks that audiences' conscious, cognition and conscious perceptions are secondary problems. According to him, the priority is to investigate how concepts that are common within large groups are reflected in daily life practices (Gerbner, 1970). Similarly, concept of society is very important for Gerbner. The quality of knowledge is integrated with consciousness of society and it includes collective idea and actions. Knowledge that is collective makes individuals aware about social identity or alienating (Gerbner, 1981). Gerbner (1970) underlined that before explaining how messages that are presented on mass media reflect the reality and how individuals react toward those messages, "collective cultivation" concept, priorities, values, and relationship between public messages on mass media should be discussed. For example, the sentences like "John believes Santa Clause" have no clear meaning till learning about which culture and when John lives, and what messages such a belief he lives in, which messages are cultivated by the public in a supportive or prohibitive way. Similarly, while interpreting about the public's point of view, many cultural indicators should be considered in the cultural heritage (Gerbner, 1969). The aim of the Cultural Indicators Project is to control and analyze real-life-related messages presented on television and their long-lasting effects. Moreover, the project defines those messages as rooted, pervasive and repetitive violence, gender stereotype, ethnicity and jobs and works (Morgan & Shanahan, 2010). With the cultivation analyses, researchers examined the audience's perception toward reality. Gerbner tried to investigate individuals' perception toward television messages. Gerbner (1970) when analyzing television messages in different dimensions, he approaches them within the framework of certain questions. The fictional messages on mass media are evaluated with their relationship between existence, priorities, values and relationships. The dimension of "existence" is related with the question of "what?." At this point, how the message takes attention of audiences, how often and how those messages are presented at mass media are core subjects that are evaluated by researchers. Within frame of this, the pervasiveness, complexity and variety of messages are also examined. In the dimension of priorities, the message is examined in what context it is important. In other words, it is important how the presentation of message is done with intensity and how the message is attributed to importance. In the dimension of values, right and wrong and good and bad concepts such as how to make valuable judgments were examined. In this context, critical and different concepts and specialties such as quality or character were evaluated. Under the last dimensions, relationships were examined. It evaluates what and how the given message is associated with, how it is constructed logically and causally. According to findings, individuals who watch television more intensely perceive real life based on messages and lessons given on television (Morgan ve Shanahan, 2010). Findings of Cultural Indicators Project showed that heavy television watching has resulted with the subjected issues like victimization, insecurity, danger and their feelings and ideas were exaggerated. Moreover, they were wrongly informed about legal and law applications in real life (Morgan & Shanahan, 2010). Within frame of research (Gerbner & Gross, 1976), heavy television viewers and light television viewers' perception toward real world and individuals were analyzed. In this context, heavy television audiences evaluate other people as if they are unreliable and danger. In the direction of those findings, Gerbner and his colleagues (1986; Morgan & Shanahan, 2010) defined the term "Mean World Syndrome." T his term is very important for media manipulation effect on children and youths. Mean World Syndrome is a tendency to perceive "real world" as more dangerous and threatening than the exact one. Of course, not every person in the real world is an angel or in every occasion is purely innocent. There are bad guys and good guys in the world. But those children and youths who suffer from Mean World Syndrome perceive that real world is too dangerous, individuals have bad intents and they always want to give harms toward other people. So, those perceptions have great impact on behaviors and perceptions toward relationships and friends of children and youths.

Fear is the most general and vulnerable to exploitation of feelings. Symbolic violence is one of the easiest ways to cultivate the minds of individuals, while violence presented ritualizing with news of crime or disaster or movies is a more risky and laborious way. More exaggerated elements and reactions are included in cases of threats or dangers in ritualized violence and against these situations. Gerbner and Gross (1976) explained this situation with individuals' exaggerated feelings of risks and unsafety. Moreover, they noted that violence on television was cultivated in the minds of individuals as social myths and that is what the church had done with stories was now done through televisions.

Media effect about reality perception and manipulate children and youths is a popular concept of media research. Studies deeply investigate children's and youths' perception toward media messages whether they are fictional or real. Findings (Cantor, 2000) showed that when children become older, they are more affected by real dangers they see on media, less affected by fictional images on media. Children who are much younger are more afraid of concepts that cannot be real, because of developmental characteristics (Monsters, alien abduction experience, etc.).

For the 21st century, Gerbner and his colleagues definitions and explanations about traditional media are valid for social and new media. Of course, the effects and implications have been changed but core discussions are same. How this social media and digital environments manipulate and shape individuals' minds?

As noted by researchers (Choi 2016; Glassman, 2012) web-based engagements are effected individuals' minds, communication styles and way to join society. In other words, digital participation and engagement enable individuals to adopt and accept new perspectives, about themselves and others. Although, as we discussed before, there are harms and risky situations about media manipulation and Mean World Syndrome, hopefully, some findings (Sestir, 2020) suggested that "Friendly World Syndrome," which means that with social media networks sites, users can develop perception toward world more positively and with trusting attitudes. But the other findings mostly stated that social media network sites have both negative and positive impact on individuals especially about the issue refugees, racism, islamophobia and misogynism (Inravia, Wolff, Paez & Gibbs, 2017; Debrael et al., 2019).

It is obvious that traditional and new media have manipulation effect on children and youths. In order to protect them from this manipulation, we must help them to strengthen their digital citizenship competence. But there are some situations on social media and in digital environment like cyber-bullying. The key point is, generally, cyber-bullying begins in the offline world then pursues cyber world or vice versa. So, this harassment is a bit different from other ones and that is the matter now we will turn.

2.2.2. Cyber-Bullying

When talking about risks and harms in digital environments most people firstly think about "cyber-bullying." Especially parents and teachers are firstly alarmed about these risks. They are not wrong because children and youths are mostly at risk about cyber-bullying. But cyber-bullying is not only related to social media consumption or talking with strangers. There are different dimensions that are more dominant about cyber-bullying such as emphatic thinking, gender, victimization of traditional and cyber-bullying, etc. So, we must analyze cyber-bullying in depth with those dimensions. Firstly, cyber-bullying could not be analyzed separated from traditional bullying.

Olweus (1991) defined bullying as harmful, repetitive and long-lasting action toward somebody or group of people. At this definition negative and harmful acts are clarified with physical, verbal or psychological behaviors. Those actions and behaviors include imbalance between victims and bullies in terms of power or force. In this context, Pepler, Craig & O'Connell, (2010) defined traditional bullying within the frame of power imbalance and aggression result from this imbalance. Addition to all definitions, bullying is kind of communication problem and disorder. Bullies learn that being perpetrator is working on increase stress, aggression and lead to control the others. Bullying is not only a simple, aggressive act but also a phenomenon with the dimensions of psychological, sociological impacts (Patchin & Hinduja; 2006). Especially on the school road, schoolyard, ground and social places like bus stations, pupils could be subject to bullying. This phenomenon, especially for youths, became a risk in terms of their social and psychological mood. As a result of this, researchers begin to study and investigate this situation (Patchin & Hinduja; 2006). But with the rise and development of Internet and technological devices, pervasiveness among pupils lead to transmit traditional bullying to cyber-bullying (Mason, 2008). So, what is cyber-bullying, which is the evolution of traditional bullying?

Cyber-bullying, which is defined as disturbing, deliberate and repeated behaviors against another individual or group via information technology tools (Mason, 2008; Li, 2006), makes parents and researchers worry about their negative impact on children and youths. Analyzing in depth, cyber-bullying includes abusive acts on online platforms, intentionally and repeatedly threatening an individual or group by sending or posting disturbing pictures, writings or graphics, (Deheu et al., 2008) or giving harm at any online platforms with any technological devices (Juvonen & Gross, 2008). Moreover, to give permission or offer opportunity to sending and spreading any disturbing, harmful messages or disclosures by themselves or others are also evaluated as cyber-bullying (Willard, 2003; Ferdon & Hertz, 2007). The major difference between cyber-bullying and traditional bullying is cyber-bullying can be done by using technological devices (Deheu et al, 2008).

Cyber-bullying is associated with many different factors, so overall findings of research may not cover every child and youth. For example, according to the different studies (Zych et al., 2019; Machackova & Pfetsch, 2016; Ang & Gog, 2010), cyber-bullying is related to empathy, anger management, low self-esteem in terms of perpetrators of cyber-bullying. This means that perpetrators are not only empathizing with their victims but also with other people while experiencing difficulties in anger control, and their self-esteem is lower than their peers.

Cyber-bullying and cyber harassment are evaluated by researchers as an ongoing problem especially for children and youths around the world (Ybarra et al., 2012; Deheu et al., 2008; Juvonen & Gross, 2008; Subrahmanyam & Greenfield, 2008; Patchin & Hinduja, 2006). The other researchers thought that cyber-bullying is inevitable at digital age (Langos, 2012; Ang & Goh, 2010).

With the development and change on social media and Internet, digital environments become vital for individuals' lives. Social media users can experience social-emotional stress because of cyber-bullying, and even they can want to remove both social media and real life (Li, 2006). Cyber-bullying is source of possible serious psychological, emotional and social disturbances (Cenat, Blais, Lavoie, Caron & Hebert, 2018; Gonzalez-Cabrera et al., 2017). When taking into consideration to developmental characteristics, those effects could lead to even suicide among teenagers due to dramatization toward most of the peer acts. Additionally, those effects increase the risks of revictimization and bullying at adulthood period (Mohammadi, Maarefvand & Hosseinzadeh, 2019; Patchin & Hinduja; 2006). Cyber-victims suffer more from depression, substance abuse (Ybarra & Mitchell, 2004), school failure, bringing sharp or dangerous tool (weapons, knives, etc.), academic unsuccessfulness, lower self-esteem and social isolation (Ybarra et al., 2007). Besides victims, cyber-bullies also suffer from depression, stress, sleep disturbances, physical and psychological problems (Aktepe, 2013; Deheu et al., 2008). Deheu et al. (2008) stated that cyber-bullying is a phenomenon that has a wide range of cases on both the perpetrators and victims from attempted suicide to murder, while Twyman et al. (2010) argued that adolescents who were engaged with cyber-bullying had social lives that are computer centered.

Risk factors that are related with cyber-bullying are generally specified with harassment, violence or sexual abuse. Those risky situations defined not to declare the intent to the victim, sending pornographic materials, verbal abuse on online environments, online thread and online sexual abuse (Berson & Berson, 2005). Moreover, problematic digital environment and Internet use are strongly related to Internet addiction and substance abuse (Gong et al., 2009), aggressive behaviors, personal problems and personality disorders, cyber-victimization and traditional peer bullying victimization (Cappadocia, 2008).

At this point, we should discuss about traditional bullying and cyber-bullying. There is strong relationship between cyber-bullying and traditional bullying (Zsila et al., 2019). Especially for pupils, victims of traditional bullying tend to be victim of cyber-bullying. Moreover, pupils who are perpetrators of cyber-bullying reported about being anonymous. Cyber-bullies admitted that anonymousness because through this anonymousness, cyber-bullying acts make them feel the power and support of bystanders. Additionally, cyber-bullies see their traditional bullying victims as easy target for cyber-bullying. Not only traditional bullies but cyber-bullies reported more personal problems and substance abuse whereas cyber-victims reported more depression and anxiety (Cappadocia, 2008). There are so many news and case studies about cyber-bullying that are published on digital and traditional media. For example, pornographic materials were sent to the e-mail of a 9-year-old girl in Australia. Her family thought that perpetrator was an adult. But after investigation of police department it is revealed that the cyber-bully was the classmate of the victim. A picture of an overweight student in Japan was secretly taken on a mobile phone while changing in the dressing room and sent to many of his friends via mobile phone (Heirman & Walrave, 2008). In September 2016, a young woman who had been leaked to the Internet during sexual intercourse in Italy had obtained the "right to be forgotten" through the judiciary, but was not able to remove abuses made about her in virtual environments and in real life and committed suicide. All the cases are of course so sad and terrible.

There are many dimensions that are related with both cyber-bullying and cyber-victimization. When research findings examined, it could be said that girls are more cyber-victims than boys, and young women are also at more risk than young men (Aboujaoude et al., 2015; Chisholm, 2006). In terms of gender differences, there is not a consensus about cyber-bullying. Some findings (Heirman & Walrave, 2008) noted that girls are more exposed to cyber-bullying than boys, and when pupils become older their risks to engage in cyber-bullying as victims or perpetrators become increased. Cyber-bullying is also related with depression. Findings showed that (Selkie et al., 2015) girls are tend to more depression whether they are engaging in cyber-bullying perpetrator or victim. The important finding is girls who are cyber-perpetrators and offered unwanted sexual relationships are more tend to depression. Unfortunately, cyber-bullying victims also tend to be subject to suicide than non-victims. Furthermore, cyber-victims have more ideas that are related with suicide and suicide attempt (Hinduja & Patchin, 2010).

Also, additional strong relationship exists with being victimization and perpetrator of cyber-bullying. It means that cyber-victims tend more to be cyber-bulling than non-victims. But traditional bullying victims tend less to perpetrator of traditional bullying than cyber-victims (Kowalski & Limber, 2007).

There are some important factors that trigger cyber-bullying in digital environments such as bystanders and nicknames in other words anonymity. Individuals or social media users who have witnessed cyber-bullying applaud, justify or approve this behavior cause cyberbullies to continue behavior and are a "bad example" for others. The rate of imitating other children and youths who have not been punished is also increasing (Barlett ve Gentile, 2012). In addition, justifying cyber-bullying also affects children's and youths' attitudes toward cyber harassment and bullying. Some study's findings showed that when university students justify cyber-bullying, students' rates of perpetrators of cyber-bullying also increased. In other words, students' justification for cyber-bullying influences their attitudes toward cyber-bullying, making it easier for them to become perpetrators of cyber-bullying in the future (Juvanen & Gross, 2008). When researchers examined the motivations of perpetrators who were cyber-bullying other children and youths, they found that they were doing it more for "revenge" (Hinduja & Patchin,2010. Not only in terms of cyberbullying but unfortunately in terms of peer bullying, which is common in schools, bullies tend to violence more while less empathy for their victims (Olweus, 1993).

Problematic online behaviors like cyber-bullying is a multilayer phenomenon and related to youths' different developmental characteristics such as identity development, peer aggression, peer rivalry, self-esteem, etc. (Jones & Mitchell, 2016) and all dimensions are related to the effects of cyber-bullying both on victims and perpetrators. That is the point now we will discuss.

2.2.2.1. Effects of Cyber-Bullying

As cyber-bullying is conducted through technological devices, different from traditional bullying, it could happen outside of the school and its effects could be more long lasting than traditional bullying (Mason, 2008).

According to Social Acceptance Model, for youths, it is very important to be popular and to continue this popularism. The damage of their self-confidence, the feeling that they are excluded or socially unacceptable by their peers can lead to many problems such as depression, academic unsuccessfulness, substance abuse or aggression (Patchin & Hinduja, 2006). Additionally, it is noted that pupils with low self-esteem are more tend to victim of repeated bullying. Similar to traditional bullying, cyber-bullying has the same consequences and if the victim does not get any support, these consequences could be turned to conduct disorder (Patchin & Hinduja, 2006). By the way, although most of the research focuses on victims' psychology and harms victims, bullies also should get support and gain awareness about the effects and definition of cyber-bullying. Moreover, like victims, cyber-bullies and online trolls also report conduct disorder or other psychological disturbances (Wang et al., 2019).

Before talking about the effect of cyber-bullying on victims, the characteristics of victims and the risky situations in terms of perpetrators and victims should be specified. As most studies' findings show (Mohammadi et al., 2019), perpetrators of traditional bullying and cyber-bullying are also victims of traditional or cyber-bullying in the past.

For risky or suspicious situations, it could be summed up as sign of peer bullying as follows: suddenly shutting down the computer when an adult or someone else enters the room while using the computer and the Internet; do not get angry, panic, when the message or e-mail is seen on the screen; be frustrated or depressed after using the computer; do not look angry and uncomfortable when you go to school or outside of the school; not reluctant to talk about what he/she was doing on the computer and suddenly broke the relationships with friends or family members. Cyber-bullies avoid talking about their actions in the digital world, use two or more e-mail accounts or user names, laugh while using computer or mobile phone and using and close several windows on the screen very fast (Diamonduros et al., 2008).

According to findings (Wang et al., 2019), cyber-victimization is strongly related to serious health and psychological issues. Additionally, researchers conclude symptoms about cyber-bullying with low self-esteem, low academic success, depression, emotional stress, violence and suicide. Besides this, even very rarely, some youths who are victims of cyber-bullying can escape from home. Moreover, victims of cyber-bullying generally show those symptoms during their adulthood period (Mason, 2008).

There are too many triggers about cyber-bullying such as traditional bullying, personal issues, ego problems, etc. But according to Strom & Strom (2005), the most important trigger of cyber-bullying is jealousy. Besides those triggers, youths generally evaluate cyber-bullying experiences as extremely upsetting, frightening and shameful. Unfortunately, some of youths try to avoid Internet usage because of those disturbing emotions (Mason, 2008) . As experts, we do not recommend to "keep away" from digital world for youths. Because the 21st century needs digitally literate citizens, digital involvement is vital for practicing their digital skills.

In terms of perpetrators, cyber-bullies do not exactly know the effect of cyber-bullying because they do not see the victims face directly unless they use webcam or skype. But, in terms of victims, the fact that the incident took place in a private area and the interpretation of the message it received increase the negative effects and damage of the event (Dehue, Bolman, & Vollink, 2008). According to findings (Juvanen & Gross, 2008), cyber-bullying has negatively great psychological impact on children and youths. Cyber-victims generally experience negative feelings such as angry and depression (Dehue et al., 2008). As normal, while youths experience those feelings they cannot want to communicate and help from their parents or teachers. Especially, youths believe their parents will ban computer or mobile phone usage if they talked about their negative experiences in the digital world. Because of this belief, they do not tell anything to anyone, and their victimization will pursue (Juvanen & Gross, 2008).

Considering all data and information about bullying and cyber-bullying, cyberbullies and cyber-victims could have psychological and emotional disorders and defects that could affect their adulthood period (Mason, 2008). So, preventing cyber-bullying due its multidimensional layouts is not easy. Now, we will turn to this phenomenon about preventing cyber-bullying.

2.2.2.2. Preventing Cyber-Bullying

Unfortunately, studies do not include hope for pupils' handling of cyber-bullying. According to findings (Li, 2010), the majority of pupils reported that they do not know what they were supposed to do when they were victim of cyber-bullying. Only 10 to 1 pupil said that they were noticed by adults or teachers. The other findings showed that (Price & Dalgleish; 2010) in terms of pupils' cyber-bullying experiences, impacts and their cope with those negative experiences, they found that 3 to 1 pupil reported that when they experienced cyber-bullying they did not want help or talk to anyone like teacher, parent or any adult.

For prevention of cyber-bullying both parents and teachers have vital roles. In order to instruct parents effectively, counselors are great sources. Firstly, school administration should cooperate with other schools, colleagues and disciplines. Schools should organize in-service trainings and all workers at school (teachers, counselors, directors, social workers and secretary) should be participate in those trainings. Moreover, pupils should join those trainings and feel free to ask questions and experiences in the digital world (Diamonduros et al., 2008). In order to prevent cyber-bullying and gain awareness about cyber-bullying, schools should consider some key points as:

1. Do not forget or underestimate the vital role of technology and digital environments on pupils' lives.

2. Gain information about potential cyber-bullying.
3. Do not forget cyber-bullies can be anonymous.
4. Do not forget that cyber-bullying can be more pervasive than traditional bullying, and victims could be bothered by different technological devices such as mobile phone, Webcam, computer, iPad, etc.)
5. Do not forget that youths will never be able to tell parents or teachers about their cyber-victimization with the idea that they will never use their mobile phone or computer again which will allow new cyber-bullying and cyber-victimization.

For effective cyber-bullying prevention program, researchers (Diamonduros et al. 2008) have advised some key points:

1. Pupils have right to feel themselves comfortable at school and home.
2. Definition of cyber-bullying.
3. How cyber-bullying is revealed.
4. The prevalence of cyber-bullying.
5. The effects of cyber-bullying on victims and perpetrators.
6. To know that electronic messages can be captured and traced.
7. Consequences of cyber-bullying.
8. Standing up against cyber-bullying.
9. To know that victims need to explain their cyber-victimization.
10. To obtain experts who work for prevention of cyber-bullying reports and support.
11. Keeping personal information confidential.
12. Internet security and digital rules.
13. To respect others when using the Internet and being responsible for the usage of technology.

Most of the researchers advise that school counselors should instruct parents on media, digital media literacy and Internet safety. Parents should set up the computers in common area in the house; they should talk with their children about cyber-bullying and its consequences. Moreover, the key point is parents should give trust to their children that they can talk with them about negative experiences in the digital world (Diamonduros et al., 2008).

As a result, even parents and sometimes governments tend to "ban" technological devices. Aktepe (2013) noted the possibility of suppressing opinions that the political authority does not approve. So, banning or forbidding the Internet and social media is a very risky situation and should not be thought of as an alternative. As a solution, digital citizenship competence of children and youths should be strengthened.

Those two harassments directly affected children and youths. But there is another common harassment for not only children and youths but also their communication and relationships with their parents, which is called "Technoference." Now, we will deeply discuss this harassment type.

2.2.3. Technoference

As technology usage has become more pervasive, researchers defined and tried to deeply investigate the effects of Technoference on parent–child communication and relationship. Generally, parents complain about their kids' technology usage and avoid communicating themselves. Moreover, intense technology usage can interfere communication between parents and kids.

Technoference is basically defined as negative effects of technological devices due to interruption of communication or interpersonal actions (McDaniel & Coyne, 2016). Unfortunately, Technoference mostly occurs in many families and it is not only related with interruption of communication. According to the findings (Roberts & David, 2015), Technoference is also related with personal well-being and attachment styles, which are basic and vital components of healthy relationships and communication. With the raise of Internet and Information technology devices, the way that families use media has also changed. When the Information technology devices were not so common, families generally were gathering around the television and watching the movies together. But in the 21st century, while sitting around television, families can also search social media network sites, read news from Internet or play digital games simultaneously. This multitasking usage habits of media has affected family functions, communication between children-youths and their parents in both positive and negative ways (Padilla-Walker, Coyne, and Fraser, 2012). As researchers noted (Livinstone et al., 2017; Baines & Gelder, 2003), media have an impact on family interactions. At this age of technology, media have an integrated role in the family. In order to strengthen family relationships, the "collective memory" is so important. By media usage, watching movie or listening to music together with family members, this collective memory would be promoted (Padilla-Walker et al., 2012). Those are positive effects of technology usage on family relationship. In terms of negative consequences, technology mostly effects leisure times of parents and their kids that they were supposed to do something together. For healthy family relationships, "leisure" times mostly seem like a perfect opportunity for chatting, talking about their daily routines, sharing experiences and developing a special language between family members. But, along with Technoference, those leisure times rely on only technology usage (McDaniel & Radesky, 2018). Besides those negative effects, other researchers (Kretz, 2019) argued about benefits of shared technology use is an opportunity for families in order to increase quality of time that they spend together. But when taken into consideration parents' usage of technology for work or spare time, it is obvious that their technology usage interfere communication with their kids. Moreover, parental technoference can lead not only kids but also teenagers to more technology usage, loneliness and increase risk of smartphone addiction for teenagers (Liu et al., 2020). So, before thinking and blaming kids and teenagers for much of using technology, maybe we could consider parents' usage of technology.

Till here, we discussed about children and youths' engagement in digital environments in terms of risks and harms. We know that controlling or punishing perpetrators or banning children and youths from using digital environments are not solution to protect children and youths from those harms. We must teach them how to protect themselves. "Digital Citizenship" is seemed valid and effective solution to protect children and youths. Now, we will deeply analyze digital citizenship.

3. Digital Citizenship

Internet and technological devices change the society in personal, educational and professional domains and social media as well. With this rapid change, digital citizenship is perceived as a coping and adaptation strategy at this fast-changing digital society's challenges. Different from digital media literacy, digital citizenship is a more inclusive and extensive skill in order to survive and benefit in digital environment. Moreover, digital citizenship is generally characterized by users' actions. Digital platform users are considered as active rather than passive individuals (Hintz et al., 2017) as media has a functional effect on construction of nation-states and laws through impact on individuals and society .

To participate in modern society needs not only consumed but also produced and created messages (Hobbs, 2010). For this reason, Hobbs (2010) stated the concept of "digital citizenship." She claimed that USA citizens should be educated about multi-media, but it should be valid for whole people all over the world. With this multi-media education, individuals gain the skills about creating media messages by using language, visual design and audio effects. In particular, media and digital media literacy education in curriculum K12 provide equal opportunities in digital media for pupils (Hobbs, 2010).

While researchers are mostly discussing about risks and harms and dark sides of the Internet and social media, they also try to present a solution for these risks. Digital citizenship is evaluated as a protection method for children and youths due to these dark sides of digital environments and defining inappropriate digital behavior throughout the world (Xu et al., 2019; Ribble & Miller, 2013).

Generally, digital citizenship competencies focus on three main subjects. First, as most of the findings show, digital citizenship competencies provide a protection against cyber-bullying and online trolling and cyber-bullying; make pupils show respectful behaviors in digital platforms; and teach how to protect privacy and intellectual property. Second, digital citizenship competencies support pupils to become digitally informed and to actively engage in digital communication and in discussion with others. Last, students with high digital citizenship skills could have a chance to actively engage in political or government-related issues, which are also necessary for both offline and online citizenship.

Digital citizenship is defined with different components that are vital for children's and youths' online behaviors not only to provide a protection for cyber harassment and cyber-bullying but also to benefit from the digital world. Jones and Mitchell (2016) addressed digital citizenship in two parts: respectful behavior online and online civic engagement. Although, the concept of digital citizenship encapsulated ethical issues about technology usage (Xu et al., 2019), it is primarily defined as the ability to navigate, exist and make sense on digital society, which is accepted as a survival tool in digital society both for work and leisure time (Emejulu & McGregor, 2019). Hintz et al. (2017) stressed the individuals' self-enactment role in society by using technological devices.

Although the researchers mostly argued about the necessity of digital citizenship, the others believe that the radical citizenship is characterized by critically analyzed consequences of technologies in everyday life and collectively constructs alternative and emancipator technologies. Moreover, radical digital citizenship reduces the effect of digital media literacy, which is vital for Internet and digital world safety. Mainly, radical digital citizenship is political practices to evaluate and understand the penetration of technology in individuals' lives (Emejulu & McGregor, 2019). For adolescences as a characteristic of developmental stage, political discussions are very attractive. So, when we try to teach and improve digital citizenship skills, we should not underestimate the impact of radical digital citizenship. Of course, adolescence have rights to express their opinion about politics but if they could not know how to recognize fake news or crosscheck what they read on digital environments, they would be fooled easily in terms of online extremism, hate speeches or gender discrimination. In terms of civic engagement under umbrella of digital citizenship, it covers the political presentation, which also seems like a risk for radical digital citizenship. But for digital citizenship education, it also covers volunteer works, supporting charities and sharing hobbies and skills (Jones & Mitchell, 2016).

Digital citizenship also takes attention of researchers in terms of education. Most of the researchers believe that in order to improve children and youths' digital citizenship skills, education is one of the best tools. Internet safety education or computer education is beneficial for awareness about risks and harms of digital environment. Ideal education for children's and youths' integration to the digital world education would be appropriate for characteristics of development and their behaviors (Jones & Mitchell, 2016), not only teaching children and youths about technology would be enough. The main aim of education for the 21st century would aim to make children and youths to participate in the digital world with higher digital citizenship competences. Moreover, with digital citizenship education pupils, online civic engagements have some outcomes for their offline civic engagement (Jones & Mitchell, 2016).

In the context of education, researchers (Choi et al., 2018) also consider teachers' digital citizenship competencies in terms of individuals' thinking, skills and behaviors relevant to Internet usage. Furthermore, not only researchers but also policy makers and educational community members believe that classroom teachers should be responsible, informed and active digital citizens. Moreover, these roles are the main goal of education (Choi et al., 2018).

When we look at the literature and educators' and policy makers' definitions and discussions about digital citizenship, we could see that the concepts of society and offline citizenship were underlined (Hintz et al., 2017; Jones & Mitchell, 2016). Moreover, digital citizenship has impact on individuals' empowering and democratizing qualifications (Hintz et al., 2017).

Born and grown up in digital age with technological devices is not enough for digital competence, which is needed for the 21st-century citizenship skills to effectively engage with the digital world (Alvermann & Sanders, 2019).

Basically, the concept of digital citizenship can be considered as ethical, responsible and safe Internet and communication devices usage (Choi et al., 2018). Although there are different subtitles, digital citizenship mainly frames with concepts of responsibility, rights, safety and security (Jones & Mitchell, 2016). Moreover, digital citizenship is examined under topics as follows: Internet safety, privacy and security, relationships and communication, cyber-bullying, digital footprints, reputation, self-image and identity, information literacy and creative credit and copyright (Jones & Mitchell, 2016). These components are described mainly under three titles: (1) Respect Yourself/Respect Others; (2) Educate Yourself/Connect with Others; (3) Protect Yourself/Protect Others (Ribble & Miller, 2013). These are separated into subtitles as digital access, digital commerce, digital communication, digital literacy, digital etiquette, digital law, digital rights and responsibilities, digital health and wellness and digital security (self-protection). All components will be discussed in depth. It is to such matters we now turn.

3.1. Respect Yourself/Respect Others

3.1.1. Digital Access

According to the reports (Rasi et al., 2019) although Internet usage rate became higher among people, most of the users connect Internet via mobile phone. This means that users could connect Internet without space or time whenever and wherever they want. In this "mediated" digital world, as noted (McGillivray et al., 2016), most of the boundaries between real and virtual became blurred. The important point for children and youths is how they perceive and react toward this blurring. What is the meaning of these digital environments for children and youths? To answering those question is vital for understanding digital accesses and enrollment of children and youths.

For the digital age, digital access not only seems like a component of digital citizenship but also seems like a right for children and youths. Furthermore, for adults, digital access and social media usage is not an option for necessity for their work (Rasi et al., 2019).

Digital access could not be considered without term of "existence." Concepts related to the "existence" of children and youths in the digital environment are initially discussed generally around lack of computer access (Deursen, 2017). Focusing on only this stage may prevent us from seeing the other problems in the cyber world. On the other hand, in order to gain awareness to children and youths for risks and harms of the digital world, first, we should not take their rights to digital access, even not threaded them; and the digital access ban should not be used as a sanction or punishment.

Digital access and participation are considered as collective actions. Individuals' engagement to the digital world makes great contribution to meaningful societal actions and political and social discussions (Atif & Chou, 2018). According to Choi et al. (2018), digital participation includes: (1) Peoples' political engagement on digital environments and (2) Personal and entertainment-centered digital participation such as digital games.

Social media and the Internet have become vital element of the individuals' lives at the 21st century. In this century, children and youths undoubtedly need to be educated about digital media and digital citizenship skills that are vital for their digital survival. Encouraging children and youths to be involved in digital environments prohibitively or constantly monitoring them will not only restrict their access rights but also disrupt their relationship between parents and children, weaken the perception of privacy and violate their personal borders. Of course, providing unlimited access to the digital world for children and youths, creating a social media profile from the moment they were born, explicitly "exhibiting" or "presenting" photos by their parents on social media network sites, YouTuber children and youths and Instamoms are also multidimensional concepts to discuss. Children and youths are particularly cyber-bullied over content on YouTube Channels or Instagram Profiles, viewers and other users often forget that they are children and expect a performance far above their development stage and the damage of their relationship with parents of children who produce content on YouTube Channel can also be considered the risks of social media for children and youths.

So how should we put "rules" on our children and youths to safely use and benefit from the Internet, to establish healthy relationships in everyday life and to prevent damage to their identity construction?

As known in order to develop and construct a healthy identity, children and youths need parents who border, set healthy and explained rules. For children's and youths' technology usage habits, 3-6-9-12 rules is advised by professionals (Tisseron, 2010; cited in Digital Media and Child, 2020). According to this rule, before 3 years any technological device (mobile phone, iPad, computer, etc.) is forbidden. It means that an early age to meet any technological device is 3 years. Six years is defined as meeting age for computer or digital games. Before age of 6, it is not advised to play digital or computer games. Nine years is the age of meeting with Internet whereas 12 years is meeting with social media. In other words, children who meet the Internet at the age of 9, search and play digital games and can begin to use social media. Of course, there would be some changes according to ages. And, of course, it is not the end of the world when a child meets with the Internet at the age of 11. But in general, children's and youths' active participation to cyber world within these boundaries will make children and youths not only digital citizens but also break away from the real world, childish stubbornness, jealousy and whims, which are the main characteristics of the developmental stage. Moreover, these boundaries also encourage children and youths to deal with conflicts not by technology but with support of their parents.

Although children and youths who are born and grown up in the 21st century are mostly familiar with digital technologies and digital environments, their parents have not kept up with changes on digital environments and mostly experience difficulties with technological devices and social media. As we said before, they are at risk groups about fake news and media manipulation and cyber-fraud. Unfortunately, because parents are not aware of the benefits of social media and focus on the risks and harms of digital media, they tend to forbid access to digital media. But if parents gain digital citizenship skills and use digital media in a conscious way, they lead their children for internet safety and conscious usage. Moreover, digital citizenship competence makes parents to learn how to deal with uncertainties of digital environments, which is the basic motivation for parents to forbid digital media. Sometimes parents are advised to monitor media activities of their children or use some rules to mediate their behavior, but literature suggests the opposite and noted that they are not always working (Daneels & Vanwynberghe, 2017).

In order to direct children and youths for conscious and safe engagement in digital environments, teachers and parents should know how to get in touch with digitally connected students (Choi et al., 2018). For this reason, policy makers and educational community members highlight that parents and teachers should be competent digital citizens. Also, Rasi et al. (2019) noted that in digitalized society most needed research is about children and youth and their relationship with media field, parents' media relations and perceptions and adults' (teacher and parents) media literacy skills (Rasi et al., 2019).

Not only accessing digital environments but also active engagement and enrolling is vital for children's and youths' development in all aspects of their lives. For example, according to findings (Baleria, 2019), story sharing among college students is very important component that support and encourage their digital media literacy skills, feeling of belonging and curiosity.

As discussed under the Digital Access section, it should be underlined that in the 21st century, at workplaces digital skills competencies provide an advantage for higher salary and attending job labor. According to findings, younger individuals have advantages for gaining digital skills than older ones. But even though older individuals could gain technical skills about media literacy, they could not develop creativity and critical thinking like younger users. This gap is not prevalent between children and youths and elder people. According to findings (Oliver & Williams-Duncan, 2019), teachers also perceive that younger pupils are more digitally competent than older pupils. Because, they claim that older pupils have more experience, and it should be considered while designing new curricula that covers digital media literacy. For older peoples it is similar. Older peoples' experiences and perceptions toward technological devices and digital environment affect their technology usage and digital technical skills (Rasi et al., 2019).

So, digital engagement has become vital for not only individual development but also participating in the labor world. Like any other skills and abilities, digital media and media literacy skills could dry up if they are not used or improved (Rasi et al., 2019). With practicing and actively engaging in the digital world, all those skills become improved and feed individuals' digital citizenship competence.

3.1.2. Digital Etiquette

Digital ethic is mainly defined as appropriate and accountable behaviors and actions in digital environments (Atif & Chou, 2018). Different from digital law, digital ethic is directly related with individuals mostly. Users in digital environments are mostly supposed to behave in an appropriate way, and they are also counted as responsible for their behaviors, have reasoning skills and cognitively mature enough to understand their behaviors' effects and results for others. But unfortunately, the reality is so different. Most of the users have those skills not only in digital environments but also in real world. And it is impossible to analyze all users' emotions or psychological moods or backgrounds about digital citizenship and ethics. Some people do not have awareness about digital ethics even they have ethic behaviors at real worlds. Especially for pupils there is another issue about this awareness. Most of the students who prepare their homework or classroom papers by copy-paste information on Internet declare that they did not know that it was crime.

Both for parents and children and youths, presenting their lives on social media network sites is not just an innocent activity but like an obligation. Unfortunately, most of the time they can ignore the ethical rules on social media network sites, such as publishing photos without permission of the picture owner. Parents publish their children's pictures, for example, innocent naked baby pictures, but the baby has the right not to want these pictures on social network sites when it becomes an adult. This is considered another ethical issue. Parents and youths should gain awareness about especially posting and sharing pictures on digital environments. As mentioned before, those pictures are also used for sexual arousal of perpetrator, although the intent of users was so innocent.

Not for other users or individuals that they know in the offline world, digital citizens are also supposed to develop ethical attitudes and behaviors to encourage responsible digital engagements within public and governmental agenda (Atif & Chou, 2018). Of course, individuals may want to share their feelings or thoughts with their surroundings on social media. It is not a case of judgment. But if those feelings and emotions are standbys for threatening or insulting targeted ones, including hate speeches, racism, social discrimination or misogynism, they are evaluated as "unethical" and for some situations they could count as a crime. It could be said that digital ethics is vital for digital citizenship and also the responsibilities of real life.

The concept of digital ethics became clear identification of different dimensions. In this context, digital ethics is examined in depth dimensions of privacy, accuracy, intellectual property and accessibility (Kert, Uz & Gecü, 2014). According to Choi et al. (2018),digital ethics are explained within the frame of three main concept: (1) ethical and responsible online behaviors, (2) awareness of cultural, political and social issues on digital environments (3) digital rights and responsibilities toward themselves and others such as cyber-bullying, online trolling or other cyber-fraud.

For all those subtitles not only children and youths but also their parents and teachers should have developed reasoning skills, emotional regulation and of course digital citizenship competence.

Now we should turn to digital law, which is mostly confused and related with digital ethics.

3.1.3. Digital Law

The definition of cybercrimes is mostly focused on a discussion: Most of the challenging behaviors on digital environments are unethical, but consequences of those unethical behaviors are punished by law and legal rules. So, definition of cybercrime is important and involved with digital ethics. Cybercrime is an umbrella term that covers activities on digital environments such as illegally accessing computer system and data, theft of intellectual property through digital mediums, sexual harassment, digital harassment, cyber-bullying, stalking and online hate speech (Holt et al., 2019). Like daily lives in the digital world, there are some rules and laws that need legal actions when somebody broke the rules and obligations. Unfortunately, among teenagers and youths mostly illegal music or film downloading is rampant activity because of structure of Internet and digital environments (Lysonski & Durvasula, 2008). This type of illegal music or film downloading is mostly counted as ethical concern, but for this book, we have discussed this issue under the umbrella of Digital Law. Although it is mostly considered as an ethical issue, the consequences are evaluated by law; moreover, illegally downloading is in violation of copyright laws. According to the findings (Lysonski & Durvasula, 2008), teenagers and youths who illegally download music, films or plagiarism on their homework or term papers mostly stressed that they did not know those actions are illegal and they need legal sanction. Moreover, the users do not consider those downloading as an unethical issue. But hopefully when teenagers and youths are informed about consequences of those downloading and fear about those consequences such as legal sanctions have an impact on illegal downloading. In other words, if youths and teenagers are informed about ethical issues and digital law, their problematic behaviors and actions are reduced in digital environments. With the rise of Internet and digital media tools, lawyers began to consider digital environments' structure that contributed to youths' and individuals' offending. Moreover, policy makers and lawyers also try to answer to questions about nature of cybercriminal and traditional criminality in terms of technology-enabled offending (Holt et al., 2019). Researchers mostly discuss cybercriminality with the frame of perception and decision making of offenders, because as we mention in media manipulation chapter, media and digital media could have impact on shaping individuals' thinking, perception and decision-making process negatively. To make clear this dilemma researchers now discuss about concept of "digital drift," which is characterized into different contents (Holt et al., 2019). Not in so many serious crimes (serial killing, brutal murder, etc.), youths seem into the risk, but in other delinquent and antisocial behaviors, youths are seemed at risk (Brewer et al., 2018).

Not only for antisocial or delinquent behaviors but also for being a conscious citizen or benefit from technological opportunities for governmental procedures, digital citizenship skills are vital. According to findings (Demirel, 2005) there is relationship between e-government applications and individuals' digital literacy competences. When e-government is applied together with necessary legal and technical infrastructure in the structure of the society with the increase information and digital literacy, the state will be effective and more efficient (Demirel, 2005).

3.2. Educate Yourself/Connect with Others

3.2.1. Digital Literacy

Media literacy skills, which have been on the agenda of researchers since 1960s, have become even more controversial, especially as children and youths are exposed to violence and pornography (Gencel-Bek ve Binark, 2010) . For the 21st century with the perception toward social media network sites as a second life place these arguments evolve toward digital media literacy and continue to be discussed.

As underlined by most of the research, digital media literacy skills (Dane els & Vanwynsberghe, 2017; Livingstone et al., 2017; Gencel-Bek & Binark, 2010) provide a protection toward risks and harms of social media such as cyber-bullying, hate speech and media manipulation. But digital media literacy skills could not be seen separate from media literacy skills.

Media literacy skills are not considered a protection method, but it would help to encourage pupils' skills and competencies to navigate and survive with modern media spaces, which evolved into digital spaces (Rasi et al., 2019).

Technological devices play a "key" role to improve individual's problem-solving abilities through media literacy skills. For adults, findings suggest that (Organization for Economic Co-Operation and Development –OECD 2016; cited in Rasi et al., 2019, p.8) technology has a facilitator effect to problem-solving abilities of adults through evaluating and analyzing information, connect and communicate with other individuals, act as appropriate for their personal, work or civic tasks and duties. Additionally, for digital environments adults with digital competence tend to use familiar applications to solve problems or get more information, which are vital for work life. In order to make pupils digitally literate, in school curriculum problem-solving skills should teach with media literacy and digital media literacy education.

Additionally, there are little differences between traditional and digital media literacies in terms of online games, mobile and online media relationships (Dezuanni, 2015).

For this reason, first we should explain media literacy skills and then digital media literacy skills.

3.2.1.1. Media Literacy

Since early childhood period, individuals have been exposed to positive/negative or wrong/right information that is spread from television, mass media or Internet. Those information sometimes reflect values about society but unfortunately mostly reflect dangers about society as explained "Mean World Syndrome" (Dezuanni, 2017). In order to protect children and youths from negative effects of media messages, studies advise media literacy skills but they noted that definition, process and application of media literacy skills could be differed by culture and society. But there is consensus about importance of media literacy and media education at information society. It is believed that media literacy education is a consequence of concern of adults and educators about children's and youths' vulnerability and being target of abuse by popular culture, television and mass media (Dezuanni, 2017).

Arguments around media literacy and digital media literacy skills mainly focus on simple question: Have we become a media literate when we know that the television environment is symbolic or taking a photo and upload on social media or texting and reading the messages on mobile phones briefly actively using social media and mass media (Potter, 2016). The researchers generally discuss how the media manipulates individuals and affects the behaviors of individuals (Potter, 2016. Both media and digital media literacy skills are recommended as a preventive skill that reduces the risks and harms of both traditional media and social media on individuals. Moreover, these skills are defined as skills that are gradually acquired, not in the short term but creating a protective effect in the long term (Livingstone, 2017). Similarly, media literacy is not an individual skill and it is not a skill to be gained in a short period of time. On the contrary, media literacy is an ideological and politically functioning process. In this context, it is necessary not to think about media literacy regardless of ideologies, politics and social processes (Gencel-Bek & Binark; 2010). Furthermore, according to the finding, most of the adults suffer from basic media literacy skills, which are now so important for work life or leisure times (Rasi et al., 2019).

Although there are so many different definitions of media literacy, the concepts focus on especially individuals' understanding of media culture and participation in this culture. In this context, media literacy is not only related to how to present stereotyped images, manipulate individuals and lead them but also related to producing media contents, which is vital for digital media literacy skills. Moreover, although media literacy is mostly considered for children and youths, due to its constructive and developing characteristics both socially and individually, it would be effective for life span (Rasi et al., 2019).

Not only it is aimed at reducing the negative effects of traditional media on individuals (violence, pornography, consumption habits, etc.), but also it is noted by the researchers that media literacy improves the critical skills, analytical thinking skills, questioning skills of individuals, and thus contributes to the fact that children and youths are conscious citizens at both digital environments and real world. Researchers studying about media literacy while explaining this concept, they consider both media knowledge and skills that could be used to produce media content as cognitive and analytic skills (Deursen, 2017). Producing digital media content also includes creative and political actions, which are also important for offline world (McGillivray et al., 2016. In addition, media literacy skills gained by children and youths are also beneficial for their cognitive development, becoming students who query and search and not memorize (Gencel-Bek & Binark, 2010). Although media literacy seems only as a skill that should be given in schools and used only at schools, media literacy skills also have significant effects on economic, social, institutional, political, health and cultural issues (Deursen, 2017). According to findings, through media literacy education, pupils are supposed to have psychological well-being, feel safer and have better competencies about self-expression and engagement to society (Rasi et al., 2019).

Although most of the research about media literacy generally focuses on children's and youths' media usage practices and pedagogy of media literacy, media literacy education should be appropriate for all ages to instruct and encourage children and youths. In terms of media literacy, as Gerbner (1970) noted, television presents a symbolic environment that mostly manipulates and destroys children's and youths' perception toward reality. Same as for the adults. But unfortunately, to protect adults and elder people from manipulative effects of media less attention is taken. Not only for children and youths but also for adults and elder people, media literacy skills are vital.

Media literacy skills encompass competencies related to analyze, evaluate and create media messages. But it is not limited with those abilities. Media literacy skills are also related with multiliteracy, news literacy and media and information literacy. Those skills are directly related to digital well-being, which is vital for a digitalized society (Rasi et al., 2019). In order to understand and analyze protective effects and advantages of media literacy, there should be more multidisciplinary approaches such as communication and media, education, psychology, sociology and human-computer interaction, and they should work together in order to provide more benefits for children and youths. Moreover, educators should apply their media contents to curriculum in order to support pupils' critical thinking and encourage them to participate in digital culture and technology (Dezunanni, 2017).

Besides all advantages (e.g., to encourage critical and analytical thinking to promote offline citizenship skills of children and youths), the vital role of media literacy is to support children's and youths' moral and cognitive developments, which are related to the protection role of digital citizenship also (Rasi et al., 2019). Through media and digital literacy education, children and youths are taught how to show appropriate behaviors in social media and analyze the discourse of inappropriate discourse on media. According to Graber & Mendoza (2012), with developmentally appropriate media literacy education, it could be possible.

Without gaining basic developmental stage characteristics such as learning fundamental skills, language acquisition, narrative acquisition, developing skeptical thinking, intensive development, experimental and active exploring, critical thinking and responsibility, effective media literacy education would not be working (Potter, 2016).

Furthermore, media literacy skill competencies also depend on cultural differences. In some cultures such as the Chinese, using bike-sharing and taxi-booking apps are very common. So, Chinese people have chance to be digitally literate (CNNIC, 2018; cited in Rasi et al., 2019: 8).

Hobbs (1999) specified questions that could work for analyzing mass media messages:

1. Who is the writer, and what is the purpose of writing?
2. What values/lifestyles/perspective did present with those messages?
3. What techniques were used to get viewers' attention?
4. What techniques were used to increase the reliability and reality of the message?
5. How do different individuals interpret this message differently?
6. What are the points that are not included in this message?
7. Who makes money from this message?

Before definition and deeply explanations of media literacy, development of media literacy should be clarified.

The first research about media literacy is presented at a conference in 1972, at Belgium, Tihange Peace University. USA, Canada, Australia and the UK have been pioneers in raising awareness and action plans of the concept of media literacy. After then whole around the world conferences were organized rapidly. Association of Media Literacy (AML) defined eight basic characteristics of media literacy skills (1987). Those characteristics are:

(1) All media products are structured.
(2) Media construct reality.
(3) Audience could evaluate media products' meanings.
(4) Media has commercial aspect.
(5) Media contains ideological and values-oriented messages.
(6) Media has social and political effects.
(7) In media messages, format and content are related.
(8) Each media tool has a special aesthetic form (cited in Jolls & Wilson, 2014:71).

In addition to all those characteristics, media education is not only related to analyzing the function of media tools or devices but also related to mass media effects on individuals' personal development and it is process related to mass media. Media education aims to create a culture that is creative, and users could evaluate media products and could have ability to self-expression using different forms of media technology. Media literacy, together with acquiring this culture, allows individuals to actively and consciously use media products such as television, radio, video, cinema, printed media and digital environments. Moreover, media literacy contains the concepts of cultural citizenship, world citizenship and media relationship (Rasi et al, 2019).

The term "literacy" in media literacy covers access to media, evaluation and media products, analyzing those media products and messages. Additionally, with media literacy skills, individuals are not passive but become active users. Media literacy is a subject that takes attention of both experts in communication and pedagogy. The basic aim of media literacy is to provide interaction between mass media and audience that should be conscious and healthy. Although there were different definitions, media literacy is defined as access, interpret and analyze information from different environments, and it covers not only traditional but also new media (Literat, 2014). According to researchers, media literacy is related to critical thinking, which is so important for cognitive and moral development of children and youths. With critical thinking skills, users can have chance to evaluate and analyze news and media products, not to believe everything that they read on the Internet and social media (Scull et al., 2014). Media literacy skills are also related to the ability to process cognitive information such as specific knowledge and awareness of rationality. In this context, media literacy skills are strongly related to choosing, interpretation and understanding the effects of media messages, communication sources and technological devices. Buckingham (2007) noted that media literacy could not be seemed like process of reading and writing, but it covers emotional reactions and enjoys cultural evaluations. Moreover, media literacy skills do not only cover evaluating media products, but also covers understanding social role of media (Hobbs, 1999). In addition, media literacy is not to keep or ban children and youths from television, Internet or mass media, but to teach the individuals to distinguish between the ability of the selecting right usage habits and the relationship of their exposure to reality by raising awareness of the effects of communication tools and media. Media literacy education is better than banning, filtering and censoring (Livingstone et al., 2017). The skills of media literacy are particularly important for children and youths to understand the relationship between imagination and reality presented in the media. In this context, it is obvious that media has not reflected the real world, but it presents real world with reshaping. As a result of this reflection, Hobbs (2010) noted that in order to effective media literacy education, this symbolic system should be resolved. According to researchers (Hobbs, 2010), media literacy and media education is necessary because it covers critical thinking abilities, which are vital for analyzing and interpreting daily media messages related to work, life and health. Media literacy researchers argue that not only individuals who understand and perceive media messages but also individuals who evaluate the messages could be grown by media literacy education (Literat, 2014). With media literacy, it is intended to create a conscious public that can read media messages correctly, analyze messages consciously and evaluate them not only on an individual's own, but also on a community-by-community level.

The increasing diversity and the possibilities by the media and the power of this diversity to influence individuals of all ages have revealed the concept of media literacy (Xu et al, 2019). Moreover, researchers argued that (Scull et al, 2014) as a consequence of gaining critical thinking abilities, media literacy is vital not only in analyzing media messages but also in increasing abilities about self-expression. Citizens who have ability to self-expression and perceive themselves as a part of democratic society have more awareness, participation and value for democratic society of course. They understand and evaluate democratic arguments and decide as a conscious citizen. Those abilities are indispensable for democratic societies. In addition, individuals with the competence of media literacy can live their lives safely and away from the images presented under the media' message bombardment. With media literacy, which allows the individuals to understand power of media to shape their thoughts, beliefs and behaviors, individuals also free from media addiction. Besides all this, media literacy helps individuals to reach different perceptions and ideas about understanding source and aim of the information (Koltay, 2011).

Media literacy is generally analyzed under two main conception (Koltay, 2011). First, with general definition, media literacy should be understood in terms of surveillance of media and how individuals and society are manipulated. In the second and problematic title, media literacy should be evaluated together with the perception skills of individuals. Accordingly, visual products from the dominant elements of media are perceived as a whole in the right hemisphere of the brain, while textual products that are more involved in traditional media are perceived by combining words and sentences in the left hemisphere of the brain. Moreover, individual's perception is influenced by their past experiences, education and emotional status. So, Natharius (2004) st ated that these two independent functions should be done together during the media literacy process and that perception skills should be used together. In this context, it could be said that media literacy has three stages: Access, understanding and meaning (Buckingham, 2007). According to other researchers (Binark & Bek, 2010) media literacy has eight stages: learning basic concepts, learning media language, learning content of media products, development of critical thinking and skepticism, deep progress, discovery, critical awareness and social responsibility.

In the most comprehensive way, not only media literacy but also media education should be defined. According to Federov (2003), media education is defined within those frameworks:

- Media education is associated with all printed, audio and textual developed with any technology and communication tools.
- Media education enables individuals to have knowledge about all the tools and means of communication they use in the community in which they live, their use and how to communicate with others through these tools.
- Through media education its aim to teach individuals those skills that cover: how to analyze, critic, and design media products; how to evaluate and interpret media products within concept of political, social, commerce or cultural values; how to choose media tool in order to reach their target audience and stories and how to reach media product in the role of both consumer and producer.

Moreover, it should be underlined that media education is a right for all citizens in all countries to express their ideas and access to information in order to construct and pursue democracy. There are other dimensions for individuals in order to reach those democratic level with media education and media research:

- To be aware of the effect of media on individuals and society,
- To understand function of mass media,
- To be able to analyze and discuss media products and messages,
- To have skills related with production and analyze,
- To have traditional and contemporary literacy skills,
- To be able to get joy from media contents, understand them and be aware of messages of media.

Researchers utilize media literacy skills not only in terms of analyze and evaluate media contents, consumer behaviors or healthy interpretation about media products and contents but also within a wide spectrum from democratic participation to gender and sex education.

Because the issues such as sex, religion or different beliefs are still a taboo, youths use Internet to get information about these issues rather than their parents and friends. Unfortunately, it is so risky for getting unhealthy and wrong information about those issues. In this context, researchers have raised the issue of sex education for youths in schools. However, the relatively low number of courses related to media literacy and digital media literacy is considered a serious deficiency in the training. With the projects like Media Aware Sexual Health (MASH) (Scull et al., 2104: 3), it is aimed to gain youths awareness about "media world" and "real world" and in doing so, media literacy skills (analyzing media texts, increasing perception of reality related to media messages, reducing the acting like media characters and increasing skepticism about media messages) are targeted. At the first part of MASH Project, researchers tried to gain basic media literacy skills to students. In this context, students learned about gender roles and stereotypes on media contents and students were informed about manipulation tactics that producers used. The second part of the project, sexuality, substance abuse and nonhealthy relationships were explained in the media world and real world. The findings showed that media literacy has positive effect on making healthy decisions about sexual behavior (Scull et al., 2014). It was a great project that proves that media literacy is not only related to analyzing and evaluating media messages. Unfortunately, in Turkey media literacy or media education lessons are not mandatory; there are elective courses at elementary schools. It seems a handicap to gain children and youths not only digital citizenship skills and competencies but also necessary skills, thinking abilities for their social lives. Society, communication researchers and educators have responsibility to protect children and youths from negative consequences and info pollution on media. For this reason, media literacy is not only related to one discipline such as communication science, but it is multidisciplined concept.

Within the pedagogical framework and developmental stages of human being and adolescence period, media literacy has positive effect on development of youths. Highlights such as heroism in media have an impact especially on youths who are trying to satisfy their sense of self-identity and are looking for personality during adolescence period. With media literacy skills at this period in which their personality is shaped, youths could have chance to differentiate negative media messages and choose messages that will have positive effect on them (Literat, 2014). From a social point of view, media literacy education provides an opportunity to students that understand how media drives politics and how television products raise public awareness (Hobbs, 1999).

Media literacy support and develop pupils' leadership skills, and environment that pupils can express themselves. Without those skills, pupils could not practice and develop problem-solving skills toward different opinions, which are vital for democratic societies (Hobbs, 1998). For environment and culture that pupils freely express themselves, media contents should be related with popular culture concepts (Hobbs, 2010) . So that, pupils could have chance to practice popular culture concepts and learn how to analyze them.

In addition to all impact such as conscious citizenship and media consumer, media literacy skills also have positive impact on protecting children and youths against violence. According to findings (Webb et al., 2010), media literacy has role to prevent violence and they create a media literacy program with the framework of eight basic questions:

(1) What are you watching?
(2) Why everybody is watching this?
(3) Violence does not solve the problems; actually it is the reason of the problems. What do you think about this?
(4) Women and Men heroes: Who is real? Who is function?
(5) How long did you watch violence?
(6) What is the main issue in this movie?
(7) Who is responsible?
(8) Time to share that you learned.

In this program, researchers noted that pupil's awareness toward violence at media increased significantly (Webb et al., 2010).

As it turns out, media literacy in general is targeted at an interaction on a social basis by creating a conscious media consumer on an individual basis. Although pupils have been studied for the most part, adults should also be more aware of media literacy education and the effects of the media. For this reason, there are some approaches toward media literacy. The core concept about media literacy approaches is to gain pupils skills and thinking abilities about asking questions while they are watching media alone (Hobbs & Frost, 2003).

The perception of reality in media is one of the basic concepts that should be considered not only in terms of media literacy, but also in terms of digital media literacy skills (Komaya, 2012; Hobbs & Frost, 2003). It will provide a better understanding of the importance of media literacy, especially how realistic and fictionally children make sense and interpret the content they see on television, cartoons or commercials from preschool (Komaya, 2012). The point to consider here is that children and youths grow up exposed to many multimedia tools in the information age. For this reason, researchers noted that children and youths can confuse reality and fiction and could not differentiate them (Komaya, 2012: 683). It is challenging enough for children to distinguish between what is happening in the real world and what is happening in the fictional media world. For this reason, children need a "passport" to understand the line between real life and fictional life and not to confuse the fictional world with the real world. This "passport" to be given to children is the teaching of media reality to children through media literacy. Therefore, the first article of approaches related with media literacy is the fact that "the media is fictional" (Komaya, 2012).

While discussing about media literacy, in literature it could be seen that individuals separated two groups as active and passive audience. The first approach, which is based on the idea that individuals should be protected against potential negative effects and harms of the media and evaluate media consumers as passive users, is called the "Protectionist Approach." In the second approach, which is described as the "Critical Media Literacy Approach," media consumers position themselves as active individuals capable of distinguishing and making decisions between the positive and negative effects of media. Although there are so many discussions about those approaches, personally I defend Critical Media Literacy Approach because with this approach children and youths' most of the skills are supported such as critical thinking, cognitive abilities, problem-solving skills and reasoning thinking skills (Hobbs, 2010).

Media literacy not only discussed with pedagogical or communication perspective but also theory of mind which is so common discussion about kids' thinking skills. Potter (2004) noted that when discussing about media literacy we should not only think about traditional views but also cognitive theories which are directly related with perception and critical thinking. In this context, according to Potter (2004) how individuals interact with media and how this interaction shapes individuals' well-being are important issues to discuss. Moreover, not only shaping the mind but also consequences of those shaping individuals' healthy or unhealthy behavior also worth discussing. Potter strongly advice media literacy education. In addition, Potter (2004) stated that relationship between society, education and media is more effective than preventive approaches. Because with effective media literacy education, individuals can learn how to filter negative and harmful messages on media.

According to researchers (Dennis, 2004), media literacy skills generally thinking mostly for elementary and high school students but when taking into consideration the general definition of media literacy covers all age groups. Moreover, universities are places where information and data about communication and media are protected, not just for youths but for the whole community. That's why media literacy education is so important for adults (Dennis, 2004).

For better media education and media literacy education, pupils should take those courses beginning from kindergarten years. Both pupils and teacher's media literacy skills should be evaluated. Findings about primary school student's media literacy skills (Bacaksız, 2010) pupils whose parents daily bought newspaper to home, have better media literacy skills than the other pupils. Moreover, media education lesson has positive impact on pupils' attitude toward newspapers and magazines. But unfortunately, factors such as not enough lesson hours for media education, families' negative attitudes toward newspapers and magazines, using inappropriate materials for media literacy lessons reduce productivity of pupils. But there were contrary research findings also (Koltay, 2011). According to findings about primary school students, there were no differences between media literate pupils and the others in terms of media watching behavior. It could be explained by developmental stage, in which pupils could not emotionally ready to auto control their media watching or using behaviors and attitudes. Moreover, according to other findings primary school pupils prefer children magazines (NG Kids, Science and Kids, etc.) than schoolbooks but those magazines have positive impact on pupils' media literacy skills (Literat, 2014).

Viewpoint of teachers and teacher candidates, there are other findings. Sometimes people think that only primary school or kindergarten teachers should have those skills. But at high school or elementary school level, all teachers should have media literacy skills. According to findings (Deveci & Çengelci, 2008), unfortunately, Social Science Teacher candidates only evaluate media literacy skills to discuss what they see or read on media with their colleagues. Moreover, they thought that their colleague's media literacy skills are not enough. Good news, although they have not enough competence, they thought they a teacher should be digitally literate. Not only for in-field-teacher candidates but also counseling teacher candidates there are great white hope findings (Kartal & Kıncal, 2012). Counseling teacher candidates were subjected to media literacy education at university. After education, they noted that their social and individual participation skills and readiness toward cognitive and emotional skills were improved, and they were linked to their perception toward media literacy education.

In order to apply effective media education, there are some key points that teachers should not ignore. They are:

(1) Advertisement, convincing and propaganda,
(2) Analyses and structure of news and fictions,
(3) Approach toward fictional storytelling,
(4) Presentation of gender, race and ideology in media message (Hobbs, 2010).

As seen, generally media literacy aims to create an interaction on a social basis by creating a conscious media consumer based on individuals. Although it is considered and underlined especially for children and youths, adults and elder people need to increase their awareness about media effect and media literacy.

Not for only pupils or youth's media literacy skills also advice for adults. Sevim (2013) examined the cover review of Elle Magazine, a medium with female representations. She stated that, patriarchal, modern and post-modern codes were blended and included in women's representations. It has also been found that the woman is usually presented as an object and this production is re-made. In this respect, Sevim (2013) offers media literacy as a solution so that female representations in popular culture can be critically evaluated by media consumers.

After penetration of digital devices to daily lives of individuals, media literacy is discussed with digital media literacy skills. With digital environments users are now not only consumers but also producers which is great function to improve media literacy skills of children and youths. For now, we should discuss digital media literacy.

3.2.1.2 Digital Media Literacy

Around the world, there are fast developments in technology, science and communication. Those changes bring radical transformations in society and alter individuals' perception toward time and space.

Along with the digital technologies are embedded in society, user's media literacy skills also need to evolve to digital media literacy skills. The necessity of learning new "literacy" skills in accordance with the nature of the digital environments has born (Deursen, 2017). Digital media literacy skills identified with two dimensions socio-material practices and reorganized knowledge about technology (Dezuanni, 2015).

When we think about the fact that social media network sites are considered as a primary source of information, the vital importance of digital media literacy skills become clearer. Before discussing about digital media literacy skills, we should explain Information literacy which is vital for checking credibility of information on Internet and social media. Generally, information literacy includes competencies for evaluating information in the digital world (Atif & Chou, 2018). According to Choi et al. (2018), information literacy includes mainly three concepts: (1) ability to access Internet (2) competences for using skills for advanced online activities and engagement

(3) psychological capabilities that include cognitive, socio-communicative and emotional abilities.

Moreover, according to researchers when used inappropriate way social media network sites could decrease students' productivity and concentration (Xu et al., 2019). With digital media literacy skills, pupils could create their own way to reach and use social media network sites.

According to researcher's media literacy and digital media literacy are very necessary abilities not only children and youths but also their parents (Comer et al., 2008). For gaining media and digital media literacy skills, family factors such as having a child is very important because parents do not choose to learn how to be digitally literate, but they get involved in the digital world to control and instruct their children. For this reason, researchers underline that due to for older and elder people are not familiar with digital media, their digital media literacy competences should go ahead with traditional media literacy skills (Rasi et al., 2019).

Researchers mostly focus on children's and youths' increasing anxiety while they are exposed to fake news, comments and violence via social media network sites. But while searching about this issue they accepted the fact that those children and youths were born in this digital environment; in other words, they are digital natives. In this context, parents are just as concerned as children and youths because, they are in an environment where they have just learned in terms of hardware and use, even though they are aware that the digital environment is not real. As a result, they are worry not only themselves but also for their children in terms of uncertainty on social media (Daneels & Vanwynsberghe, 2017). However, parents' higher media literacy and digital media literacy skills also have positive contributions to their children. In an experimental study, videos and news about possible future terrorist attacks were shown to youths aged 7–13 and their mothers. According to findings, mothers with high media and digital media literacy skills were less anxiety and stressed. In addition, older youths also saw these videos and news as a more social threat than younger youths. Mothers who have high media literacy skills were more support their children in terms of calm down and reduce their anxiety (Comer et al., 2008).

Digital literacy skills encompass some focus groups such as ability to access, survive, navigate and produce in the digital world. However, digital media literacy skills do not only relate with computer and Internet based skills but also with critical, analytical, and computational thinking skills which are so vital for offline citizenship and daily life. For this reason, researchers now advice Coding to integrate education curricula in order to encourage pupils' computational thinking abilities and gain to them technical perspectives toward computational mechanism which are also related with digital media literacy education (Rasi et al., 2019).

Digital media literacy also important for psychological well-being because, it support individuals to search how to take social support from social media networks. Also, digitally literate users know how get contact from digital environment while do not lose the control and subject to abusive behaviors. Findings related to teacher's usage of media literacy tools, it was found that this tool improve teachers critical and analytical thinking (Blanton et al., 2019). Moreover, practices with this tool teachers feel more confident about media literacy education and supervise, encourage pupils. Regarding this finding, it is suggested that teachers should engage different digital tools and environments actively in order to instruct pupils.

As underlined before, digital games have positive impacts on children's learning and engaging digital environments. Digital games like Minecraft, which are centered on digital block constructions and designs and produced a digital environment, offer an opportunity for children to strengthen their digital media literacy skills. The important dimension of digital media literacy skill is producing a digital content which could be done by online games or actively using social media network sites (Dezuanni, 2018; Banks & Potts, 2010).

Producing media content presents a metaphor that stands for individuals, and technology should work and go ahead in order to create meaning and practices. Basically, technology and individuals should not be separated. Only technological developments could not work for humans in terms of meaning or soul. As said by the researchers, "Human are not machine." They cannot be considered as a mathematical equity or they cannot be as predictable as 100 %. But, unfortunately, in the 21st century most of the people behave as if humans are machine. Mostly individuals' need to find "meaning" in technology. So, while producing media content, of course technological devices are vital but without human it is not mean anything. For adults and elder people, beside exceptions, it seems impossible to create digital environments fully appropriate for children. Because older people are now "digital immigrants," there should be some inappropriateness with them and children. But, if children and youths learn how to construct and create digital environments and contexts for digital games, social media network sites or vlogs, it would be better to address their peers. Moreover, as Dezuanni (2018) suggests, if children's digital game experiences are analyzed in terms of their performance, collaboration with others and experiences, researchers can better understand how children apply their digital media literacy skills. Theoretically, children and youths can learn digital media literacy skills but as follow up they must evaluate and control in terms of their application of those skills in digital environments. The question that must be answered is "Can children and youths turn their theoretical knowledge into practice?" In order to answer this question first, children and youths' social interactions and experiences in digital environments should deeply analyzed. Secondly, the role and intervention of parents are also examined. Too much interventions would be harmful for children, but some digital environments do not permit parent or adult intervene. It is also not appropriate for children and youths' digital experiences. Thirdly, as technical part, the quality and quantity of hardware and software must be evaluated. Lastly, in order to improve children and youths' digital media literacy skills educators and policy makers should enrich their conceptual digital resources (Dezuanni, 2018).

As noted by researchers (McGillivray et al., 2016) digital media literacy skills seem like important social skills for children and youths to survive not only digital environments but also in offline world. But, for reaching this aim, digital literacy skill programs and curriculum should be designed to prepare children and youths to fully participate society and community (Alvermann & Sanders, 2019).

The contemporary culture of the 21st century is called "Information Society"; and in this context, the results arising from the interaction between technological tools and humans often affect the perceptions and life practices of individuals, while in particular they cause cultural and pedagogical changes (Goodova et al., 2015). Those changes and their effects could be evaluated within the frame of convenience in communication, the increased performance of workers, and improvements in health services, data flow, and a sustainable environment (Daly, 2000). Simultaneously and in many ways, technology has divided and reshaped the old and stereotyped fields of individuals' lives. With this point of view, developments in digital technologies have first become industrialized then become visible in individuals' social lives (Castells, 2008). In the world, digital cultural groups increasingly being created across the borders. Research also tend to focus on information and communication technologies, and their consequences such as ne economics, new working cultures, and new economics as result, new working cultures and new opportunities for individuals' spare times. Those studies are focus on how technology effects the society and culture, and their relationship with technology. As to popular media, it is argued that technology is center of the social changes and independent from society. Penetration, usage and impact of technology depend on social, economic dimensions and Internet policies of countries (Daly, 2000). At this point before examining digital media literacy skills of pupils, Technological Determinism Theory should be explained.

The most fundamental idea of Technological Determinism Theory is that communication between individuals shapes the existence of humanity. In this context, an invention in information and communication technology leads to cultural change. First, the tools are shaped by humans, then the tools begin to shape the people and society (Baytun & Özerem, 2012). In short, at the Theory of Technological Determinism, it is claimed that technology shapes the society by social practices such as learning (Oliver, 2011). It is also stated that this shaping effect of technology on society causes changes in attention, learning or even brain structures on the part of individuals (Oliver, 2011).

There are some other arguments about Technological Determinism Theory. Dafoe (2015) noted that technological determinism is a causal approach that defines technology or technological tools and is at the center of the social change process. Moreover, they explain the theory with domino effect. At this point of view, technology causes something than as a result of this many intermediary steps are influenced. This process affects the whole social process from specific to general. For example, it can be suggested that the invention of the car caused the reduction in price of foods. Because the automobile has reduced the need for horses, which can be considered to lead to a decrease in horse manger grains, which is an increase in areas appropriate for farming for consumable food, which in this situation has led to reduced food prices. But the main problem in this "portrait" is there are no humans. Technological determinists argue that human factor emerges only when needed (Croteau & Hoynes, 2000). In other words, there are structural rules and there are no human actions. Therefore, society is transformed into "technique" not according to people's needs.

In discussions about technological determinism, researchers define the labels and definitions made by separating them from the general and technology characteristics of technology rather than practices (case studies focusing on practices in social life) (Oliver, 2011). New technologies reshape ingrained habits and cultural practices (Croteau & Hoynes, 2000). In this context, it is not enough to ask only what new technologies do to people in order to make sense of the relationship between the media and society; at the same time, researchers thought individuals should be asked what they are doing with new technology.

There are deep discussions about relationship between media and new technologies (Castells, 2008). Researchers argued that function of technology in terms of social changes. Technology can lead changes in society but not "only" technology can achieve it. There should be additional factors and dimensions such as users' decisions, options and attitudes toward technology. Those additional factors are not easily controlled by technology or society. It resulted with unpredictability of technological changes and acceptance of technology. Moreover, harms and benefits of technology are not clear and consistent. Like this idea, Derry (2007) noted that individuals generally think about technological devices more than social practices, meaning and information in context of technology. Oliver (2011) evaluated technological determinism as "optimistic" and "pessimistic" ones. According to this evaluation, developments are rapid and make it easy for individuals' lives labeled as "optimistic technological determinism," whereas if those rapid developments lead to idea that humans are in danger in terms of losing their jobs those are labeled as "pessimistic technological determinism." But it is accepted that technology is the reason for changing in society, and the fact that these changes are optimistic or pessimistic differentiations is according to whether society wants change or not (Oliver, 2011). Castells (2008) technology is one of the most important driving forces of social change. With this driving force, basic habitats and forms of relationship are undergoing rapid change. With these forms, the meanings given to society and socialization begin to change. The main source of social meaning production for society is the socialized communication process. In this context, socialized communication also happens beyond inter-personal communication in the public sphere. According to Avcı (2015) as a result of rising technology and its penetration to individuals' lives, it is easier for them to be audited and checked and become consumption objects. Moreover, with digital environments, individuals' lives become digitized. In this context, individuals express themselves quantitatively in new media environments, which makes them easier to observe and Avcı (2015) stated that digital environments bring a different dimension to classical sociology theories. In addition to this idea, Krug (2005) noted that technology evolves in the world in which people live, while at the same time changing their perceptions and thoughts, and in this way, the symbols in their worlds diversify. According to Krug (2005), this situation could simply explained with theory of technological determinism. It could be explained with meaningful structure and conceptual functioning of technology in depth.

"New" literacies are important in terms of they include evolution at digital and media technologies; also, it affects expectations from work and private lives of individuals. This new literacy in other words digital media literacy includes innovative text formats (such as multimedia or hybrid text), the expectations of new users/readers (nonlinear readings, animations, etc.) and new activities (website design, creation, production, etc.) (Barone & Wright, 2008).

With digitalization, media has gained features such as intractability, virtuality and modularity. Because of those characteristics, media consumers have gone from passive to active. Digital environments where media consumers are actively involved also continue to develop as an international social network that is open, transparent, easy to reach and easy to create, free from concepts such as space and time, most importantly enabling virtual identities. With a rapid penetration of Internet to individuals' lives, it also brings so many transformations and changes. In particular, understandings and applications about traditional communication have started to take place in the digital environment, and in this context, users have become both producers and consumers of information (Volkenburg & Cantor, 2001).

Media literacy has taken a path from content to digital tools, and therefore the concept of "digital literacy" should be defined. Active engagement in digital environments requires special and different competences and those competences are evaluated independent from content (Park, 2012). Media and digital media literacy concepts should be framed with culture, media education, human-computer interaction and social works related to technology (Livingstone, 2004).

There is incomprehensibility about the term "new" media. The term new stands for transformation at media, not opposed of "old". Faster, global and portable information and communication devices enable transformation of interpersonal communication to mass communication. It is seen that information that can be connected to each other by the hypertextivity feature of the new media can move continuously on high-speed data networks and respond to users' demands (Özel, 2012:).

Media literacy is generally defined with the discussions such as is media literacy so different from digital media literacy or media literacy should be transformed to Internet or computer literacy (Buckingham, 2007; Livingstone, 2004). Another discussion such as skills, analyze and critical thinking that are needed for both media and digital media literacy shaped the discussions into other ways. For better digital media literacy skills, children and youths should have some competences such as multi-tasking, collective intelligence, reasoning, analytical thinking and idea exchange (Rasi et al, 2019). So, we could say that both media and digital media literacy skills are not only related to watching television and using social media or communication devices.

In terms of digital media literacy, the user's role is defined again as both consumer and producer (Literat, 2014). Moreover, user's role in digital environment is not limited with sharing content or communicating with others; they are also subjected to digital activism and multi-media construction when their digital literacy skills become better. They are volunteer and tend to active participation in society through digital environments (Literat, 2014). Increasing accessibility is resulted with change in communication types and media contents. With regard to this fact, it is necessary to raise awareness of the production of messages and media contents, thinking that everyone can produce media.

Researchers see online pornography not only as an individual but also a society-related problem. For this reason, researchers advises for children and youth digital media literacy in order to protect them from harmful effects of pornography. Youths and teenagers mostly seek about romantic relationships on social media and digital environments; and unfortunately, those relationships have risks about fool, fraud, lying, physical and emotional abuse (Waheed, 2019).

The main dimensions about digital media literacy especially emerge while pupils create a media product. When creating products, students reflect not only their digital media literacy skills but also the "cyber culture" in which they live. Many digital software programs are specifically designed for professionals. Therefore, the digital products that pupils create are limited to either their parents' digital media literacy experiences or what they learn from social media sites. At this point, for both media and digital media literacy, there is a key word that became invisible: accessibility. For media products, that pupils produce factor of accessibility is only a beginning point. Accessibility is not only to evaluate as reaching information and communication devices, it also covers users' cultural norms, self-expression and communication skills. Moreover, those skills and dimensions could be changed depending on individuals (Buckingham, 2007).

3.2.2. Digital Communication

Due to characteristic of adolescence period, it is known that for healthy development of children and youths, they need to communicate and bound relationship with others. Through involving in digital environments and online communication, youths have chance to construct or support their healthy development.

About digital engagement of youths, some old studies argue that most of youths use digital communication in order to strengthen their offline relationship (Valkenburg & Peter, 2007). But according to the research after 2015, most of the youths noted that they can connect and communicate with strangers on digital environments (Chan, 2020; Waheed, 2019). Youths also believe that they feel comfortable when they express themselves to their friends on digital environments (Liu et al., 2019; Valkenburg & Peter, 2007). Researchers underline that youths' communications with strangers in digital environment mostly related to cultural and individual differences. According to findings (Valkenburg & Peter, 2007) of research conducted by 600 youths, participants reported that their online friendships have different motivations related to their characteristics. Extrovert youths noted that they communicate online because they express themselves easily. On the other hand, introverted youths reported their online communication motivation as their offline social relationships are weak.

With the development and pervasiveness of technological devices, children and youths have a chance to meet and talk with strangers. Meeting or talking with is very risky situation. With the perception of children and youths, they claim that meeting with strangers is not different thing than meeting someone in school beginning of the semester. It is not the same or similar situation meeting someone in Internet, because we know that most of the perpetrators or psychopaths generally use Internet and social media to hunt their victims. So, not with mostly control and limited children and youths' Internet and social media usage, but with gain them consciousness about usage of digital environments we should teach them to protect themselves in digital environments.

Children and youths could use digital environments with different purposes and motivations. Sometimes they use technological devices and social media to share their daily experiences and sometimes they see digital environments as alternative for face-to-face communication especially during Covid-19 Pandemic. Moreover, most of the youths reported that they feel psychologically better than their offline communication (Subrahmanyam & Greenfield, 2008), especially in romantic relationships or flirting, youths reported that they prefer online communication (Lykens et al., 2019). Those purposes and motivations sometimes evolve to positive or negative consequences of digital environments. For example, on social media, youths sometimes discuss hot topics and learn new things about the world, and it supports their social development, but sometimes they get exposed to hate speeches or gender discriminations (Subrahmanyam & Greenfield, 2008). In order to protect them from that violence, as educators and parents, we should inform them about the risks to meet a stranger from Internet. Before talking with youths and teenagers about talking to strangers on Internet, parents firstly should build a healthy relationship and communication with their children. Before building this type of healthy relationship, discussions about risks of Internet would be useless. Moreover, those discussions would have effect to direct youths to meeting strangers on

Internet. Additionally, youths' motivation about online communication is related to reduce their getting bored, and to improve lack of their social life. Pupils who have permanent online friends less tend to talk with strangers (Peter, 2006).

Some children and youths are more digitally connected than the other ones. Those children and youths who are more digitally connected have some characteristics, experiences and thinking. Being more digitally connected especially creates risky situations for cyber harassment. Moreover, personal characteristics of youths who communicate online with strangers are very important. This type of communication and online interactions are also risky and dangerous if the stranger is older than the youth or gloating.

When examined further studies, youths who have mental issues, psychologically vulnerable or have problems that are special to developmental characteristics tend to communicate online with strangers. Moreover, they bound more closely with this relationship. Additionally, youths who have parental issues tend to online talk with strangers. If youths have difficulty with communication, they also tend to talk with strangers. Youths with complex moods spend more time in digital environments, often chatting and talking with strangers (Wolak et al., 2003).

Using digital environments make easier both youths' and adults' daily lives and vital for daily routines (Berson & Berson; 2005). Besides negative consequences, digital environments, online friendships and talking with strangers have also some positive consequences. Some findings showed that youths who communicate online with strangers reported less social exclusion. Moreover, talking online with strangers supports a sense of belonging, especially for vulnerable teenagers. As known, forums, blogs or social media network sites are not only used for communication but also used for exchanging opinions, general discussions, and getting informed about some vulnerable or risky subjects.

It is obvious that the nature of electronic communication makes chances for social communication and relationships of individuals; youths and teenagers mostly prefer online communication, and it effects their social, cognitive and identity development and characteristics.

3.2.3. Digital Commerce

For the digital environment, the most obvious fact is children and youths are not only digital consumers but also producers in digital environments (McGillivray et al., 2016). Their involvement in digital environments as producer and consumer is mostly affected by attitudes and perceptions, which is explained with "media effect." The effects of mass media on individuals' attitude, behaviors and beliefs are studied and investigated by social psychology fields, advertisement departments and public relationships . But for children there is a bit difference. Before the age of 5, according to Piaget, who is a Swiss developmental psychologist, children do not mature enough for reasoning. They are also not mature enough to differentiate what is function and what is reality. So, they are appropriate "hunting" for advertisements. Because they mostly believe what they watch in the advertisements, and they are potential consumers for firms. Moreover, their consumer behaviors which start at early ages could pursue to older ages also (Valkenburg & Cantor, 2001).

Digital commerce is mostly discussed with focus on the consumer information of children and youths. Mainly, the marketers try to analyze and collect personal information as children and youth consumers. But that information is also considered as a defect for the privacy of children and youths. Because we are living "datafied" environment consumer actions and behaviors as children and youths are important for companies and firms. Digital fraud and digital misleading mostly cover the financial loss or credit card cheat; the big problem for children and youths is their private consumer behaviors or digital footprints that could be used by others or sold to companies or firms. Not only our private information but also our many activities data-geo-location, smart cities and homes where are fulfilled with sensors, metadata of our online communication is stored, monitored, shared and sold by social media services. Of course, those monitoring could have some benefits for digital users with targeted advertising or personalized data that may offer convenience (Hintz et al., 2017).

Internet and new media technologies enable media consumers, active participants and media producer. When considered as the importance of full participation in digital environment, it has become a frequently debated topic of how much the importance of media literacy has increased and how important it is for critical media consumption and responsible media production (Literat, 2014).

3.3. Protect Yourself/Protect Others

3.3.1. Digital Rights and Responsibilities

For policy makers, the penetration of technological devices and social media networks sites on individuals' lives is a hot topic in terms of collection, distribution and manipulation of personal data and concept of privacy (Norberg et al.,

2007). To teach children and youths how to protect their and others' rights, we must teach them to consider "privacy" on digital environments. Since the infancy period, parents try to teach the concept of privacy and how to protect themselves from strangers. Now, for the information age, parents try to do same thing to their children. Like protecting themselves from strangers, children and youths should have ability and be conscious to protect themselves from strangers, trolls and perpetrators on digital environments.

Effective use of digital environments and social media could encourage and enhance active participation in society, innovation, social change and offline citizenship and strengthening active citizenship as well (Hintz et al., 2017). By effective educational practices, both offline and distance education, we could reshape the role of digital education in order to encourage digital citizens who perform their online responsibility in a democratic society (Atif & Chou, 2018).

While pupils gain responsibility about their online actions, they gain also more control on their online engagement. In order to control or reduce cyberbullies and online trolls and to teach pupils responsible online engagement, taking responsibility of their online activities seems an appropriate way.

In order to actively integrate pupils to the digital world, they should be informed about their role to pursue conversations and behaviors in digital environments. The vital note is pupils should gain awareness about possibility that sometimes in the digital world things will go wrong. It is not such a big problem and most of the time it will be solved (Ciccone, 2019).

As a characteristic of digital environment, users have a chance to share personal information that is defined as one of the ways to construct and pursue relationships both online and offline. But while discussing about communication and relationships' engagement with digital environment, researchers mostly focus on the concept of self-disclosure of information. Self-disclosure of information seems like an important issue because most of the social media networks site users have reported that they are worried about their online violation of their privacy (Hallam & Zanella, 2017). But, on the contrary of the worries and anxieties of users about privacy, most of the users give information about their privacy on social network sites. There is a gap between users' worries about privacy protection, and privacy-related behavior is labeled as a "privacy paradox" (Norberg et al., 2007). Digital media users mostly give importance to benefits of sharing information instead of considering potential risks of sharing private information or photos (Hallam & Zanella, 2017).

3.3.2. Digital Security (Self-Protection)

This subtitle is related to the other subtitle of digital citizenship directly. When we teach children and youths basic "mentality" of digital citizenship, they would automatically begin to think to protect themselves in digital environment. Because, they will know that they can benefit from digital environments while protecting themselves. It would not something strict or fearful for them. But unfortunately, digital security is mostly learned haphazardly.

Most of the digital media users do not have credible sources to lead them about risks, dangers and dark sides of the Internet and the digital environment. Unfortunately, instead of trustworthy sources, children and youths turn toward less credible sources such as media, workplace and the stories of negative experiences that have happened to acquaintances (Redmiles et al., 2016) . In order to instruct children and youths for conscious and safe Internet and social media practices, parents should have digital media literacy skills and digital citizenship competence (Daneels & Vanwynsberghe, 2017). When they direct and lead children and youths to secure Internet usage and model them, it would be easier for them.

Moreover, children and youths sometimes need to help to release their anxiety about Internet and digital environment. If parents and teachers are appropriate model for them, they can calm down and enjoy to digital environments. If they only informed about harms and risks of the Internet and digital environments, as normal, they can try to avoid technology and Internet.

3.3.3. Digital Health and Wellness

One of the important components of digital citizenship is digital health. Digital health is defined as "Using Information and computer technologies in the process of diagnosis and treatment of patients, monitoring the health and risk status of non-patients, training health care workers and in controlling and improving public health" (Turkish Cardiology Association- Digital Health Project Group, 2020). At this part digital health is explained and discussed in terms of the effects of social media usage habits of children's and youths' body image perception, and health communication with their parents about healthy foods and healthy nutrition and exercises in order to protect their body posture while using technological devices.

Digital health and its applications mostly discussed in terms of elder people and according to findings (Eronen et al., 2019), elder people have difficulty with evaluating, analyzing and judging news about health on media and social media. In order to benefit from health news on media, social media individuals should have health literacy also (Eronen et al., 2019). Although health literacy is commonly considered to protect elder people to fraud about health issues on digital environments, it is also advised for children and youths as potential consumers of health information and services related with body image and physical appearances of children and youths. Related with this issue, health literacy skills become vital. Health literacy is defined as ability to analyze and evaluate health applications and news (Manofo & Wong, 2012). For effective health literacy, children and youths also should be informed about infodemic, which is spreading false news or misinformation during pandemic (Eysenbach, 2011; Eysenbach, 2002). During the Covid-19 pandemic, unfortunately both elders and youths experienced infodemic and it increased their anxiety.

The other negative consequence related with digital health is "comparing," which is so dangerous to individuals' well-being. Social media users tend more to compare themselves and their lives with other users (Fox & Vendemia, 2016). Moreover, girls photoshop more their photos than boys, and girls feel worse when they compare themselves at social media. Body image perception and physical acceptance play an important role about those comparisons (Cohen et al., 2019).

Conclusion

We should renew education system, and it should be appropriate for growing pupils with better digital citizenship skills and competences. Hybrid education models that include skills and competence toward improving pupils' digital citizenship awareness and competence would be a solution to protect children and youths from the risks and harms of digital spaces. Moreover, social media usage, awareness toward fake news, Deep-Fake and manipulations should be gained by Hybrid Education System.

Parents are also an important dimension for effective digital citizenship competence. Parental involvement has a disincentive effect on risky and inappropriate online behaviors of children and youths. In my opinion, threatening children and youths with "law" or "rule" is not effective protection method for inappropriate or harmful behaviors. As adults, educators, researchers and parents, first, we must improve our digital citizenship competence and then guide and instruct children and youths for safe involvement in digital environments.

I want to finalize this book with the phrase that I conclude to all my seminars to high school students: People are not computers. When you close your computer, you do not close the people that you chat with.

References

Abad, L. (2014). Media Literacy for Older People Facing the Digital Divide: The E-inclusion Programs Design, Comunicar: Media Education Research Journal, Vol. 21, No. 42, pp: 173–180.

Abbasi, I.S. (2019). Social Media Addiction in Romantic Relationships: Does User's Age Influence vulnerability to Social Media Infidelity?, Personality and Individual Differences, Vol. 139, pp: 277–280.

Aboujaoude, E., Savage, M.W., Starcevic, V. & Salame, W.O. (2015). Cyberbullying: Review of Old Problem Gone Viral, Journal of Adolescent Health, Vol. 57, pp: 10–18.

Ahn, J. (2011). The Effect of Social Network Sites on Adolescents' Social and Academic Development: Current Theories and Controversies, Journal of American Society for Information Science and Technology, Vol. 62, No. 8, pp: 1435–1445.

Aktepe, E. (2013). Cyberbullying and Cybervictimization among Adolescents, New Symposium Journal, Vol. 51, No. 1, pp: 31–36.

Alvermann, D.E. & Sanders, R.K. (2019). Adolescent Literacy in a Digital World, The International Encyclopedia of Media Literacy, Renee Hobbs and Paul Mihailidis (Editors-in-Chief), John Wiley & Sons, Inc.

Amedieu, F., Salmeron, L., Cegarra, J., Paubel, P.V., Lemarie, J. & Chavalier, A. (2015). Learning from Concept Mapping and Hypertext: An Eye Tracking Study, Vol. No. 4, pp: 100–112.

Ang, R.P. & Goh, D.H. (2010). Cyberbullying Among Adolescents: The Role of Affective and Cognitive Empathy and Gender, Child Psychiatry Hum Dev, Vol. 41, pp: 387–397.

Ashiekpe, A.J. & Ugande, G.B. (2017). Analysis of the Effects of Social Media Sexting on Adolescents and Youths Sexual Behaviors and Attitudes Towards Sexuality in Nigeria, International Journal of Innovative Research and Advanced Studies (IJIRAS), Vol. 4 Issue 1, pp: 227–232.

Atif, Y. & Chou, C. (2018). Digital Citizenship: Innovations in Education, Practice and Pedagogy, Journal of Educational Technology & Society, Vol. 21, No. 1, pp: 152–154.

Bacaksız, T. (2010). Using Newspaper and Magazines in Media Literacy Education: The Effects of Media Literacy Education on Students' Newspapers and Magazine Readings, Unpublished Master Thesis, Gazi University Ankara.

Baines, S. & Gelder, U. (2003). What Is Family Friendly about the Workplace in the Home? The Case of Self-Employed Parents and Their Children, New Technology, Work and Employment, Vol 18, No 3, pp: 3223-234.

Baleria, G. (2019). Story Sharing in a Digital Space to Counter Othering and Foster Belonging and Curiosity among College Students, Journal of Media Literacy Education, Vol. 11, No. 2, pp: 56-78.

Banks, J. & Potts, J. (2010). Co-creating Games: A Co-evolutionary Analysis, New Media & Society, Vol. 12, No. 2, pp: 253-270.

Barlett, C.P. & Gentile, D.A. (2012). Attacking Others Online: The Formation of Cyberbullying in Late Adolescence. *Psychology of Popular Media Culture*, Vol. 1, No. 2, pp: 123-135.

Barone, D. & Wright, T.E. (2008). Literacy Instruction with Digital and Media Technologies, The Reading Teacher, Vol. 62, No. 4, pp: 292-302.

Baytun, İ.D. & Özerem, A. (2012). Education in the Grip of Technological Determinism Concept, International Journal of New Trends in Arts, Sports & Science Education, Vol. 1, No. 4, pp: 45-53.

Benedikter, R. & Fitz, N. (2011). Technophilia and the New Media: Contemporary Questions of Responsible Cultural Consumption, a Call for Public Debate, Synesis: A Journal of Science, Technology, Ethics and Policy, pp: G62-G68.

Berson I.R. & Berson, M.J. (2005). Challenging Online Behaviors of Youth. Social Science Computer Review, Vol. 23, No. 1, pp:29-38.

Binark M. & Gencel-Bek, M. (2010). Critical Media Literacy-Conceptual Approaches and Applications, Kalkedon Publication, İstanbul.

Blanton, M.V., Cheek, A.E. & Bellows, E. (2019). Real-Time Support: Using eCoaching to Increase Preservice Teachers' Confidence to Teach, Journal of Media Literacy Education, Vol. 11, No. 2, pp: 179-188.

Bocij, P. (2004). Cyberstalking: Harassment in the Internet Age and How to Protect Your Family. Praeger Publication: USA.

Boyd, D. (2014). It's Complicated: The Social Lives of Networked Teens. Yale University Press: London.

Brewer, R., Cale, J., Goldsmith, A. & Holt, T. (2018). Young People the Internet, and Emerging Pathways into Criminality: A Study of Australian Adolescents, International Journal of Cyber-Criminality, Vol. 12, No. 1, pp: 115-132.

Buckingham, D. (2007). Digital Media Literacies: Rethinking Media Education in the Age of the Internet, Research in Comparative and International Education, Vol. 2, No. 1, pp: 43-55.

Canet, J.M., Blais, M., Lavoie, F., Caron, P.O. & Hebert, M. (2018). Cyberbullying Victimization and Substance Use Among Quebec High Schools Students: The Mediating Role of Psychological Distress, Computer in Human Behavior, Vol. 89, pp: 207-212.

Cappadocia, M.C. (2008). Cyberbullying and Cybervictimization: Prevalence, Stability, Risk and Protective Factors and Psychosocial Problems, York University, Master of Thesis, Toronto-Canada.

Castells, M. (2008). The New Public Sphere: Global Civil Society, Communication Networks, and Global Governance, The Annals of the American Academy of Political and Social Science, Vol. 616, No 1, pp: 78-93.

Chan, G.H. (2020). Intimacy, Friendship, and Forms of Online Communication Among Hidden Youth in Hong Kong, Computers in Human Behaviors, Vol. 111, pp: 1-7.

Chan-Olmsted, S., Cho, M. & Lee, S. (2013). User Perceptions of Social Media: A Comparative Study of Perceived Characteristics and User Profiles by Social Media, Online Journal of Communication and Media Technologies, Vol. 3, No. 4, pp: 149-178.

Chen, Y.R. & Schultz, P.J. (2016). The Effect of Information Communication Technology Interventions on Reducing Social Isolation in the Elderly: A Systematic Review, Journal of Medical Internet Research, Vol. 18, No. 1, pp: 1-18.

Cheng, J.W., Mitomo, H., Otsuka, T. & Jeon, S.Y. (2016). Cultivation Effects of Mass and Social Media on Perceptions and Behavioral Intentions in Post-disaster Recovery – The Case of the 2011 Great East Japan Earthquake, Telematics and Informatics, Vol. 33, pp: 753-772.

Chisholm, J. F. (2006). Cyberspace Violence Against Girls and Adolescent Females, Annals New York Academy of Sciences, Vol. 1087, pp: 74-89.

Choi, M. (2016). A Concept Analysis of Digital Citizenship for Democratic Citizenship Education in the Internet Age, Theory & Research in Social Education, Vol. 44, No. 4, pp: 565-607.

Choi, M., Cristol, D. & Gimbert, B. (2018). Teachers as Digital Citizens: The Influence of Individual Backgrounds, Internet Use and Psychological Characteristics on Teachers' Levels of Digital Citizenship, Computer & Education, Vol. 121, pp: 143-161.

Ciboci, L. (2019). Representation of Children and Youths in Media, The International Encyclopedia of Media Literacy. Renee Hobbs and Paul Mihailidis (Editors-in-Chief), Gianna Cappello, Maria Ranieri, and Benjamin Thevenin (Associate Editors). JohnWiley & Sons, Inc.

Ciccone, M. (2019). Teaching Adolescents to Communicate (Better) Online: Best Practices from a Middle School Classroom, Journal of Media Literacy Education, Vol. 11, No. 2, pp: 167–178.

Cohen, R., Fardouly, J., Newton-John, T. & Slater, A. (2019). #Bopo on Instagram: An Experimental Investigation of the Effects of Viewing Body Positive Content on Young Women's Mood and Body Image, New Media & Society, Vol. 21, No. 7, pp: 1546–1564.

Comer, J.S., Furr, J.M., Beidas, R.S., Weiner, C.L. & Kendall, P.C. (2008). Children and Terrorism-Related News: Training Parents in Coping and Media Literacy. Journal of Consulting and Clinical Psychology, Vol. 76, No. 4, pp: 568–578.

Coşkun, Y.D., Kızılkaya, G.C. & Seçkin, H. (2013). Computer Technology Teacher Candidates' Views on the Concepts of Literacy Related to Information Technology, International Journal of Human Sciences, Vol. 10, No. 1, pp: 1259–1272.

Cranwell, J., Whittamore, K. John Brinton, J. & Leonardo-Bee, J. (2016). Alcohol and Tobacco Content in UK Video Games and Their Association with Alcohol and Tobacco Use Among Young People, Cyberpsychology, Behavior and Social Networking, Vol. 19, No. 7, pp: 426–434.

Dafoe, A. (2015). On Technological Determinism: A Typology, Scope Conditions, and a Mechanism, Science, Technology, & Human Values, Vol. 40, No 6, pp: 1047–1076.

Daly, J.A. (2000). Studying the Impacts of the Internet Without Assuming Technological Determinism, Aslib Proceedings, Vol. 52, No. 8, pp: 285–301.

Daneels, R. & Vanwynsberghe, H. (2017). Mediating Social Media Use: Connecting Parent's Mediation Strategies and Social Media Literacy, Cyberpsychology: Journal of Psychosocial Research on Cyberspace, Vol. 11, No. 3, pp: 1–13.

Debrael, M., d' Haenens, L. & De Cock, R. (2019). Media Use, Fear of Terrorism, and Attitudes Towards Immigrants and Refugees: Young People and Adults Compared, The International Communication Gazette, pp: 1–21.

Deheu, F., Bolman, C. & Völlınk, T. (2008). Cyberbullying: Youngsters' Experiences and Parental Perception, Cyberpsychology & Behavior, Vol. 11, No. 2, pp: 217–223.

Demirel, D. (2005). E-government as a Means of Effective State and Turkish Public Administration, Unpublished Master Thesis, Kocaeli University, Kocaeli.

Dennis, E.E. (2004). Out of Sight and Out of Mind: The Media Literacy Needs of Grown-Ups, American Behavioral Scientist, Vol. 48, No. 2, pp: 202–211.

DePaula, N., Dincelli, E. & Harrison, T.M. (2018). Toward a Typology of Government Social Media Communication: Democratic Goals, Symbolic Acts and Self-presentation, Government Information Quarterly, Vol. 35, pp: 98–108.

Derry, J. (2007). Epistemology and Conceptual Resources for the Development of Learning Technologies, Journal of Computer Assisted Learning, Vol. 23, pp: 503–510.

Deveci, T. & Çengelci, H. (2008). A look the media literacy by Social Studies teacher candidates. Yüzüncü Yıl University Journal of Education Faculty, Vol. 5, No. 2, pp: 25–43.

Dezuanni, M. (2015). The Building Blocks of Digital Media Literacy: Sociometrical Participation and the Production of Media Knowledge, Journal of Curriculum Studies, Vol. 47, No. 3, pp: 416–439.

Dezuanni, M. (2017). Agentive Realism and Media Literacy, The Journal of Media Literacy, Vol. 64, No. 1-2, pp: 16–19.

Dezuanni, M. (2018). Minecraft and Children's Digital Making: Implications for Media Literacy Education, Learning, Media, and Technology, Vol. 43, No. 3, pp: 236–249.

Dezuanni, M., Beavis, C. & O'Mara, J. (2015). Redstone Is Like Electricity: Children's Performative Representations in and Around Minecraft, E-Learning and Digital Media, Vol. 12, No. 2, pp: 147–163.

Diamonduros, T., Downs, E. & Jenkins, S.J. (2008). The Role of School Psychologist in the Assessment, Prevention and Intervention of Cyberbullying Psychology in the Schools, Vol. 45, No. 8, 683–704.

Dreßing, H., Bailer,J., Anders, A., Henriette Wagner, H. & Gallas, C. (2014). Cyberstalking in a Large Sample of Social Network Users: Prevelance, Characteristics and Impact Upon Victims, Cyberpsychology, Behavior and Social Networking, Vol. 17, No. 2, pp: 61–67.

Emejulu, A. & McGregor, C. (2019). Towards a Radical Digital Citizenship in Digital Education, Critical Studies in Education, Vol. 60, No. 1, pp: 131–147.

Eronen, J., Paakkari, L., Portegijs, E., Saajanaho, M. & Rantanen, T. (2019). Assessment of Health Literacy Among Older Finns, Aging Clinical and Experimental Research, Vol. 31, No. 4, pp: 549–556.

Eysenbach, G. (2002). Infodemiology: The Epidemiology of (Mis)information, The American Journal of Medicine, Vol. 113, pp: 763–765.

Eysenbach, G. (2011). Infodemiology and Infoveillance Tracking Online Health Information and Cyberbehavior for Public Health, American Journal of Preventive Medicine, Vol. 40, No. 5S2, pp: 154–158.

Eysenbach, G. (2020). How to Fight an Infodemic: The Four Pillars of Infodemic Management, Journal of Medical Internet Research, Vol. 22, Issue 6, pp: 1–6.

Fox, J. & Vandemia, M.A. (2016). Selective Self-Presentation and Social Comparison Through Photographs on Social Networking Sites, Cyberpsychology, Behavior and Social Networking, Vol. 19, No. 10, pp: 593–600.

Gans, H.J. (2014). The American News Media in an Increasingly Unequal Society, International Journal of Communication, Vol. 8, pp: 2484–2495.

Gencer, Z.T. (2012). A Practical Study on the Role of Social Entropy in the Process of Creating Agenda of the Media, Unpublished Doctorate Thesis, Konya.

Gerbner, G. (1970). Cultural Indicators: The Case of Violence in Television Drama. The Annals of the American Academy of Political and Social Science, Vol. 388, No. 1, pp: 69–81.

Gerbner, G. & Gross, L. (1976). Living with Television, Journal of Communication, Spring, Vol. 26, No. 2, pp: 172–199.

Gerbner, G., Gross, L., Morgan, M. & Signorielli, N. (1981). Scientists on the TV Screen, Culture and Society, May/June, pp: 41–44.

Glassman, M. (2012). An Era of Webs: Technique, Technology, and the New Cognitive (R) evolution, New Ideas in Psychology, Vol. 30, pp: 308–318.

Gong, J., Chen, X., Zeng, J., Li, F., Zhou, D. & Wang, Z. (2009). Adolescent Addictive Internet Use and Drug Abuse in Wuhan, China, Addiction Research & Theory, Vol. 17, No. 3, pp: 291–305.

Goodova, M., Rubtsova, E. & Fernandez, R.F.F. (2015). Multimedia Resources as Examples of Polymorphic Educational Hypertexts in the Post-Literacy Era, Procedia, Social and Behavioral Sciences, Vol. 214, pp: 952–957.

Graber, D. & Mendoza, K. (2012). New Media Literacy Education (NMLE): A Developmental Approach, Journal of Media Literacy Education, Vol. 4, No. 1, pp: 82–92.

Hallam, C. & Zanella, G. (2017). Online Self-Disclosure: The Privacy Paradox Explained as a Temporally Discounted Balance Between Concerns and Rewards, Computers in Human Behavior, Vol. 68, pp: 217–227.

Heirman, W. & Walrave, M. (2008). Assessing Concerns and Issues about the Mediation of Technology in Cyberbullying, Journal of Psychosocial Research on Cyberspace, Vol. 2, No. 2, Article 1.

Hinduja, S. & Patchin, J.W. (2010). Bullying, Cyberbullying and Suicide, Archives of Suicide Research, Vol. 14, pp: 206–221.

Hintz, A., Dencik, L. & Wahl-Jorgensen, K. (2017). Digital Citizenship and Surveillance Society, Internation Journal of Communication, Vol. 11, pp: 731–739.

Hobbs, R. (2010). Digital and Media Literacy: A Plan of Action, The Aspen Institute Communications and Society Program. Washington, D.C.: The Aspen Institute.

Hobbs, R. (1999). The Seven Great Debates in the Media Literacy Movement, To The Educational Resources Information Center (Eric), Opinion Notes.

Hogan, B. (2010). The Presentation of Self in the Age of Social Media: Distinguishing Performances and Exhibitions Online, Bulletin of Science, Technology & Society, Vol. 30, No. 6, pp: 377–386.

Hogue, J.V. & Mills, J.S. (2019). The Effect of Active Social Media Engagement with Peers on Body Image in Young Women, Body Image, Vol. 28, pp: 1–5.

Holt, T.J., Brewer, R. & Goldsmith, A. (2019). Digital Drift and the "Sense of Injustice": Counter-Productive Policing of Youth Cybercrime, Vol. 40, No. 9, pp: 1144–1156.

Huesmann, L. R. (2007). The Impact of Electronic Violence: Scientific Theory and Research, Journal of Adolescent Health, Vol. 41, pp: S6–S13.

James, C. & Cotnam-Kappel, M. (2020). Doubtful Dialogue: How Youth Navigate the Draw (and Drawbacks) of Online Political Dialogue, Learning, Media and Technology, Vol. 45, No. 2, pp: 129–150.

Jenkins, H. & Deuze, M. (2008). Convergence Culture Convergence: The International Journal of Research into New Media Technologies, Vol. 14, No. 1, pp: 5–12.

Jolls, T. & Wilson, C. (2014). The Core Concepts: Fundamental to Media Literacy Yesterday, Today and Tomorrow, The National Association for Media Literacy Education's, Journal of Media Literacy Education, Vol. 6, No. 2, pp: 68–78.

Jones, L.M. & Mitchell, K.J. (2016). Defining and Measuring Youth Digital Citizenship, New Media & Society, Vol. 18, No. 9, pp: 2063–2079.

Juvonen, J. & Gross, E.F. (2008). Extending the School Grounds?—Bullying Experiences in Cyberspace, Journal of School Health, Vol. 78, Issue 9, pp: 496–505.

Kafai, Y.B. & Peppler, K.A. (2011). Youth, Technology and DIY: Developing Participatory Competencies in Creative Media Production, Review of Research in Education, Vol. 35, pp: 89–119.

Kara, T. (2011). An Examination About Visual Media Effects on Family Members, Unpublished TUİK Thesis, Ankara.

Kartal, O.Y. & Kıncal, R.Y. (2012). Factors That Influence Active Citizenship Levels Of Psychological Counseling And Guidance Department Students Who Received Media Literacy. M.U. Atatürk Faculty of Education, Journal of Educational Sciences, Vol 36, pp: 169–191.

Kert, S.B., Uz, Ç, & Gecü, Z. (2014). Effectiveness of an Electronic Performance Support System on Computer Ethics and Ethical Decision-Making Education, International Forum of Educational Technology & Society, Vol. 17, No. 3, pp: 320–331

Koltay, T. (2011). The Media and the Literacies: Media Literacy, Information Literacy, Digital Literacy, Media, Culture & Society, Vol. 32, No. 2, pp: 211–221.

Kowalski, R.M. & Limber, S.P. (2007). Electronic Bullying Among Middle School Students, Journal of Adolescent Health, Vol. 41, No. 6, pp: S22–S30.

Laar, E.V., Deursen, A.J.A.M.V., Dijk, J.A.G.M.V. & Haan, J.D. (2017). The Relation Between 21st-century Skills and Digital Skills: A Systematic Literature Review, Computers in Human Behavior, Vol. 72, pp: 577–588.

Langos, C. (2012). Cyberbullying: The Challenge to Define, Cyberpsychology, Behavior and Social Networking, Vol. 15, Issue 6, pp: 285–289.

Li, Q. (2006). Cyberbullying in Schools: A Research of Gender Differences, School Psychology International, Vol. 27, No. 2, pp: 157–170.

Li, Q. (2010). Cyberbullying in High Schools: A Study of Student's Behaviors and Beliefs About This New Phenomenon, Journal of Aggression, Maltreatment & Trauma, Vol. 19, pp: 371–392.

Literat, I. (2014). Measuring New Media Literacies: Towards the Development of a Comprehensive Assessment Tool, Journal of Media Literacy Education, Vol. 6, Issue 1, pp: 15–27.

Livingstone, S. (2004). Media Literacy and the Challenge of New Information and Communication Technologies, The Communication Review, Vol. 7, No. 1, pp: 3–14.

Livingstone, S., Olafsson, K., Helsper, E.J., Lupinaz-Villanueva, F., Veltri, G.A. & Folkvord, F. (2017). Maximizing Opportunities and Minimizing Risks for Children Online: The Role of Digital Skills in Emerging Strategies of Parental Mediation, Journal of Communication, pp: 1–24.

Liu, Q., Huang, J., & Zhou, Z. (2020). Self-Expansion Via Smartphone And Smartphone Addiction Tendency Amongadolescents: A Moderated Mediation Model, Children and Youth Service Review, Vol. 119, No. 105590, pp: 1–9.

Lykens, J., Pilloton, M., Silva, C., Schlamm, E., Wilburn, K. & Pence, E. (2019). Google for Sexual Relationships: Mixed-Methods Study on Digital Flirting and Online Dating Among Adolescent Youth and Young Adults, JMIR Public Health and Surveillance, Vol. 5, No. 2, pp: 1–8.

Lyon, D. (2017). Surveillance Culture: Engagement, Exposure, and Ethics in Digital Modernity, International Journal of Communication, Vol. 11, pp: 824–842.

Lysonski, S. & Durvasula, S. (2008). Digital Piracy of MP3s: Consumer and Ethical Predispositions, Journal of Consumer Marketing, Vol. 25/3, pp: 167–178.

Machackova, H. & Pfetsch, J. (2016). Bystanders' Responses to Offline Bullying and Cyberbullying: The Role of Empathy and Normative Beliefs About Aggression, Scandinavian Journal of Psychology, Vol. 57, pp: 169–176.

Manafo, E. & Wong, S. (2012). eSEARCH: A Tool to Promote the eHealth Literacy Skills of Older Adults, Journal of Consumer Health on the Internet, Vol. 17, No. 3, pp: 255–271.

Mason, K.L. (2008) Cyberbullying: A Preliminary Assessment for School Personnel. Psychology in The School, Vol. 45 No. 4, pp: 323–348.

McDaniel, B.T. & Radesky, J.S. (2018). Technoference: Longitudinal Associations Between Parent Technology Use, Parenting Stress, And Child Behavior Problems, Pediatric Research, Vol. 84, pp: 210–218.

McDaniel, B. T., & Coyne, S. M. (2016). "Technoference": The Interference Of Technology In Couple Relationships And Implications For Women's Personal And Relational Well-Being, Psychology of Popular Media Culture, Vol. 1, pp: 85–98.

McGillivray, D., Mcpherson, J., Jones, J. & McCandlish, A. (2016). Young People, Digital Media Making and Critical Digital Citizenship, Leisure Studies, Vol. 35, No. 6, pp: 724–738.

McGrath, M.M. & Casey, E. (2002). Forensic Psychiatry and the Internet: Practical Perspectives on Sexual Predators and Obsessional Harassers in Cyberspace, Journal of the American Academy of Psychiatry and the Law, Vol. 30, pp: 81–94.

McLean, S.A., Jarman, H.K. & Rodgers, R.F. (2019). How Do "Selfies" Impact Adolescents' Well-being and Body Confidence? A Narrative Review, Psychology Research and Behavior Management, Vol. 12, pp: 513–521.

Medina, M., Coyle, W. & Rodriguez, A. (2014). Project Facebook Honduras: The Construction of the Socail Reality of Honduran University Youth on Facebook, https://www.semanticscholar.org/paper/

Project-Facebook-Honduras%3A-The-Construction-of-the-Medina-Coyle/a41d104b4476cf91f0e9988f56e598be0aae8c9b?p2df

Middaugh, E. (2019). More Than Just Facts: Promoting Civic Media Literacy in the Era of Outrage, Peabody Journal of Education, Vol. 94, No. 1, pp: 17–31.

Mohammadi, A., Maarefvand, M. & Hosseinzadeh, S. (2019). Effectiveness of Cognitive Behavioral Social Work Intervention on Preventing Cyberbullying Revictimization Among Youths. Quarterly Journal of Social Work, Vol. 8, No. 1, pp: 5–13.

Morgan, M. & Shanahan, J. (2010). The State of Cultivation, Journal of Broadcasting & Electronic Media, Vol. 54, No. 2, pp: 337–355.

Moshfegh, N. & Ebrahimi, P. (2018). Elementary School Students, The Anonymous Victims of Cyberbullying, Proceedings of SOCIOINT 2018-5th International Conference on Education, Social Sciences and Humanities, 2-4 July 2018- Dubai, U.A.E.

Narmanlıoğlu, H. (2016). Television Images and Social Reality, Turkish Studies, International Periodical for the Languages, Literature and History of Turkish or Turkic, Vol. 11, No. 2, pp: 935–950.

Norberg, P.A., Horne, D.R. & Horne, D.A. (2007). The Privacy Paradox: Personal Information Disclosure Intentions Versus Behaviors, The Journal of Consumer Affairs, Vol. 41, No.1, pp: 100–126.

Oliver, K.M. & Williams-Duncan, S. (2019). Faith Leaders Developing Digital Literacies: Demands and Resources across Career Stages According to Theological Educators, Journal of Media Literacy Education, Vol. 11, No. 2, pp: 122–145.

Oliver, M. (2011). Technological Determinism in Educational Technology Research: Some Alternative Ways of Thinking About the Relationship Between Learning and Technology, Journal of Computer Assisted Learning, Vol. 27, pp: 373–384.

Olweous, D. (1991). Victimization Among School Children, Advances in Psychology, Vol 76, pp: 45–102.

Padilla-Walker, L., Coyne, S.M. & Fraser, A.M. (2012). Getting a High-Speed Family Connection: Associations Between Family Media Use and Family Connection, Family Relations, Vol. 61, pp: 426–440.

Park, S. (2012). Dimensions of Digital Media Literacy and the Relationship with Social Exclusion, Media International Australia, No. 142, pp: 87–100.

Patchin, J.W. & Hinduja, S. (2006). Bullies Move Beyond the School Yard: Youth Violence and Juvenile Justice, Vol. 4. No. 2. pp: 18–169.

Pellicone, A. & Ahn, J. (2015). Building Worlds: A Connective Ethnography of Play in Minecraft, Games and Culture, Vol. 13, No. 5, pp: 440–458.

Peng, S., Yang, A., Cao, L., Yu, S. & Xie, D. (2017). Social Influence Modeling Using Information Theory in Mobile Social Networks, Information Sciences, Vol. 379, pp: 146–159.

Pepler, D., Craig, W. & O'Connell, P. (2010). Peer processes in bullying: Informing prevention and intervention strategies. In S. R. Jimerson, S. M. Swearer, & D. L. Espelage (Eds.), Handbook of bullying in schools: An international perspective (p. 469–479). Routledge/Taylor & Francis Group.

Potter, J.W. (2004). Argument for the Need for a Cognitive Theory of Media Literacy, American Behavioral Scientist, Vol. 48, No. 2, pp: 266–272.

Potter, W.J. (2016). Media Literacy (8th ed.). USA: SAGE PUBLICATION.

Price, M. & Dalgleish, J. (2010). Cyberbullying: Experiences, Impacts and Coping Strategies as Described by Australian Young People, Youth Studies Australia, Vol 29, No. 2, pp: 51–59.

Rasi, P., Vuojarvi, H. & Ruokama, H. (2019). Media Literacy and Education for All Ages, Journal of Media Literacy Education, Vol. 11, No. 2, pp: 1–19.

Redmiles, E.M., Kross, S. & Mazurek, M.L. (2016). How I Learned to be Secure: A Census-Representative Survey of Security Advice Sources and Behavior, CCS'16, October 24–28, Vienna, Austria.

Reed, L.A., Tolman, R.M. & Ward, L.M. (2016). Snooping and Sexting: Digital Media as a Context for Dating Aggression and Abuse Among College Students, Violence Against Women, Vol. 22, No. 13, pp: 1–21.

Ribble, M. & Miller, T.N. (2013). Educational Leadership in an Online World: Connecting Students to Technology Responsibly, Safely, and Ethically, Journal of Asynchronous Learning Networks, Vol. 17, No. 1, pp: 137–145.

Saud, M., Ida, R., Abbas, A., Ashfaq, A. & Ahmad, A.R. (2020). The Social Media and Digitalization of Political Participation in Youths: An Indonesian Perspective, Society, Vol. 8, No. 1, pp: 83–93.

Schultz, F., Utz, S. & Göritz, A. (2011). Is the Medium the Message? Perceptions of and Reactions to Crisis Communication via Twitter, Blogs and Traditional Media, Public Relations Review, Vol. 37, pp: 20–27.

Scull,T.M., Malik, C.V. & Kupersmidt, J.B. (2014). A Media Literacy Education Approach to Teaching Adolescents Comprehensive Sexual Health Education, Journal of Media Education, Vol. 6, No. 1, pp: 1–14.

Seidman, G., Roberts, A. & Zeigler-Hill, V. (2019). Narcissism and Romantic Relationship Presentation on Social Media: The Role of Motivations and Partner Attractiveness, Personality and Individual Differences, Vol. 149, pp: 21–30.

Şeker, T. & Şimşek, F. (2012). Reception Analysis of the Effect of "Muhteşem Yüzyıl" TV Series on High School Students in the Context of Encoding/Decoding, Communication Journal of Selçuk, Vol. 7, No. 2, pp: 111–120.

Selkie, E.M., Rajitha, K., Chan, Y.F. & Moreno, M. (2015). Cyberbullying, Depression and Problem Alcohol Use in Female College Students: A Multisite Study, Cyberpsychology, Behavior and Social Networking, Vol. 18, No.2, pp: 79–86.

Sestir, M.A. (2020). This Is the Way the World "Friends": Social Network Site Usage and Cultivation Effects, The Journal of Social Media in Society, Vol. 9, No. 1, pp: 1–21.

Strom, P. & Strom, R.D. (2005). When Teens Turn Cyberbullies. Education Digest: Essetial Readings Condensed for Quick Review, Vol. 71, Issue 4. pp: 35–41.

Subrahmanyam, K. & Greenfied, P. (2008). Online Communication and Adolescent Relationships. The Future of Children, Vol. 18, No. 1, pp: 119–148.

Sugihartati, R. (2019). The Identity Fragmentation of Youths as Fans of Global Popular Culture, Pertanika Journals Social Sciences & Humanities, Vol. 27, No. 2, pp: 1007–1022.

Tisseron, S. (2010). 3-6-9-12 Rules https://dijitalmedyavecocuk.bilgi.edu.tr/2020/03/11/3-6-9-12-yas-kurali-cocuklarin-yasina-gore-uygun-elektronik-cihaz-kullanimi/ Access at 07.12.2020.

Tüzel, S. & Tok, M.M. (2013). Examining Teacher Candidate's Digital Writing Experiences, Journal of History School, Year 6, No. XV, pp: 577–596.

Twyman, K., Saylor, C., Taylor, L.A. & Comeaux, C. (2010). Comparing Children and Adolescents Engaged in Cyberbullying to Matched Peers, Cyberpsychology, Behavior and Social Networking, Vol. 13, No. 2, pp: 195–199.

Valenzuela, S., Arriagada, A. & Scherman, A. (2012). The Social Media Basis of Youth Protest Behavior: The Case of Chile, Journal of Communication, Vol. 62, No. 2, pp: 1–16.

Valkenburg, P. & Peter, J. (2007). Preadolescents and Adolescents' Online Communication and Their Closeness to Friends. Developmental Psychology, Vol. 43, No. 2, pp: 267–277.

Valkenburg, P.M. & Peter, J. (2011). Online Communication Among Adolescents: An Integrated Model of Its Attraction, Opportunities and Risks, Journal of Adolescent Health, Vol. 48, Issue 2, pp: 121–127.

Valkenburg, P.M. & Cantor, J. (2001). The Development of a Child into a Consumer, Journal of Applied Developmental Psychology, pp: 61–72.

Waheed, M. (2019). Online Threats And Risky Behaviour From The Perspective Of Malaysian Youths, SEARCH Journal of Media and Communication Research, Vol. 11, No. 2, pp: 57–71.

Wang, Z., Xie, Q., Xin, M., Wei, C., Yu, C., Zhen, S., Liu, S., Wang, J. and Zhang, W. (2019). Cybervictimization, Depression, and Adolescent Internet Addiction: The Moderating Effect of Prosocial Peer Affiliation, Frontiers in Psychology, Vol. 11, pp:1–9.

Wariya, J.D. (2016). A Language of Play: New Media's Possibility Spaces, Computers and Composition, Vol. 40, pp: 32–47.

Webb, T., Martin, K., Afifi, A. & Kraus, J. (2010). Media Literacy as a Violence-Prevention Strategy: A Pilot Evaluation, Health Promotion Practice, Vol. 11, No. 5, pp: 714–722.

Willard, N. (2003). Off-Campus, Harmful Online Student Speech, Journal of School Violence, Vol. 2, Issue 1, pp: 65–93.

Wolak, J., Mitchell, K. & Finkelhor, D. (2003). Escaping or Connecting? Characteristics of Youth Who from Close Online Relationships, Journal of Adolescence. Vol. 26, No. 1. pp: 105–119.

Xu, S., Yang, H.H., MacLeod, J. & Zhu, S. (2019). Social Media Competence and Digital Citizenship Among College Students, Convergence: The International Journal of Research into New Media Technologies, Vol. 24, No. 4, pp: 735–752.

Ybarra, L.M., Boyd, D., Korchmaros, J.D. & Oppenheim, J.K. (2012). Defining and Measuring Cyberbullying within the Larger Context of Bullying Victimization, Journal of Adolescent Health, Vol. 51, pp: 53–58.

Ybarra, L.M., Mitchell, J.K., D. & Wolak, J. (2007). Internet Prevention Messages: Targeting the Right Online Behaviors, Archives of Pediatrics & Adolescent Medicine, Vol. 161, 2007, pp: 138–145.

Ybarra, L.M. & Mitchell, J.K. (2004). Online Aggressor/Targets, Aggressors, And Targets: A Comparison Of Associated Youth Characteristics, The Journal of Child Psychology and Psychiatry, Vol. 45, No. 7, pp: 1308–1316.

Yeo, T.E.D. & Chu, T.H. (2017). Sharing "Sex Secrets" on Facebook: A Content Analysis of Youth Peer Communication and Advice Exchange on Social Media about Sexual Health and Intimate Relations, Journal of Health Communication, Vol. 22, No. 9, pp: 753–762.

Zolkepli, I.A. & Kamarulzaman, Y. (2015). Social Media Adoption: The Role of Media Needs and Innovation Characteristics, Computers in Human Behaviors, Vol. 43, pp: 189–209.

Zsila, A., Urbán, R., Griffiths, M.D. & Demetrovics, Z. (2019). Gender Differences in the Association Between Cyberbullying Victimization and

Perpetration: The Role of Anger Rumination and Traditional Bullying Experiences, The International Journal of Mental Health and Addiction, Vol. 17, pp: 1252–1267.

Zych, I., Baldry, A.C., Farrington, D.P, & Llorent, V.J. (2019). Are Children Involved in Cyberbullying Low on Empathy? A Systematic Review and Meta-analysis of Research on Empathy Versus Different Cyberbullying Roles, Aggression and Violent Behavior, Vol. 54, pp: 83–97.

www.ingramcontent.com/pod-product-compliance
Ingram Content Group UK Ltd.
Pitfield, Milton Keynes, MK11 3LW, UK
UKHW021324180426
11947UKWH00017B/1415